Perfect Phrases™ for Writing Job Descriptions

Hundreds of Ready-to-Use Phrases for Writing Effective, Informative, and Useful Job Descriptions

Carole Martin

D0368179

New York Chicago San Francisco Lisbon
London Madrid Mexico City Milan New Delhi
San Juan Seoul Singapore Sydney Toronto

*The **McGraw·Hill** Companies*

Copyright © 2010 by Carole Martin. All rights reserved. Printed in the United States of America. Except as permitted under the United States Copyright Act of 1976, no part of this publication may be reproduced or distributed in any form or by any means, or stored in a database or retrieval system, without the prior written permission of the publisher.

1 2 3 4 5 6 7 8 9 0 FGR/FGR 0 1 0 9

ISBN: 978-0-07-163560-8
MHID: 0-07-163560-2

This book is printed on acid-free paper.

McGraw-Hill books are available at special quantity discounts to use as premiums and sales promotions, or for use in corporate training programs. To contact a representative please e-mail us at bulk-sales@mcgraw-hill.com.

To seven very special people in my life:
Joshua Noorda
Alby Noorda
Nicholas Patyk
Annie Rose Patyk
Dylan Patrick Hurd
Kate Alexandra Patyk
Lily Madison Hurd

Contents

Contents

Contents

Contents

Introduction

The job description is to the job what the foundation is to the house.

Every structure begins at the bottom with a strong foundation on which to build. Like a structure's foundation, a well-written job description can be used as the basis to establish and build the expectations of the job.

When writing a job description you lay the groundwork for a particular job and for your relationship with the person you hire to do the work. When you first put in a requisition for a new person, you begin to build the justification for the position and what you expect the person who fills this position to do within the department or organization.

Sometimes a requisition will include only the essentials of why you need to add to the head count or to replace a person who is leaving. In a requisition you are usually trying to obtain approval from a source for the funding of this new person's salary. You will need to include information and facts about why you are adding this new person and how the addition of staff will improve the performance or the results of projects or objectives for your department.

Once you obtain the head-count approval, you will need to expand upon your original idea for the position and begin to think of exactly what you want and need from this new hire in order to deliver on what you have promised in your requisition or request.

This book will take you through the steps of building your job description and how to use it to justify, define, and refine the purpose of this job. You can then use this information in your job posting, in the preparation for your interview questions, and for the communication that will take place after the new hire joins the organization.

Longer term, this job description can be used as a performance measure to assess progress and achievements of the new employee against set objectives.

Taking the time to write a comprehensive job description will save time and money. These are some of the benefits to be reaped:

- *The job description can be used in the course of the recruitment process.* Writing a job posting will become easier and clearer if you take the time to define exactly what you are looking for in a candidate.

- *It will become an essential tool to use in hiring the right candidate.* You will not find what you are looking for unless you know exactly what you want in a candidate. Once you have defined the definition and requirements of the job, you will find interviewing and judging candidates to be much more focused and, as a result, a more objective process.

- *It may be used as a communication tool to bridge the gap between the supervisor or manager and the new employee from the interview to the first day of employment.* The job description can be used when setting expectations and objectives in your first meeting with the new employee. Setting goals and objects from the beginning of a person's employment gives the person a sense of direction of where he or she should be going and how to get there.

■ *It will be one of the greatest assets you can use to judge performance and give feedback to the new employee about progress and behavior.* Often taking care of small problems can avoid larger problems in the future. Performance management will be a less dreaded process if it is done on an ongoing basis. When the yearly chore of writing up performance appraisals rolls around, your job as manager will be virtually done if you have followed a systematic method of regular meetings and regular feedback.

How a Well-Written Job Description Can Assist You

Recruitment

Defining the position in detail and writing it in an interesting and stimulating manner will help attract the types of candidates you want. Once the résumés begin to come in, the job description and the standards set for the position will assist you in the process of weeding out the candidates who don't quite have what it takes from the candidates in whom you are interested. This way you will not waste your time or the candidate's time by interviewing people who either cannot do the job or who will not fit into the department or organization.

Introduction

As a source of recruitment, the job description will help you formulate the questions to ask when screening the résumé, doing a phone screening, or conducting a formal interview. When the expectations and needs are clear, it is far easier to realize what questions to ask the candidate and then know what to listen for in the answers given. Without a job description the hiring person is functioning blindly, using subjective feelings to dominate the hiring decision.

Once the factors are spelled out in the job description, they can be used to write a "help wanted" ad or job posting. The job description can be used as a guide to relate what the requirements of the position are so that both the interviewer and the candidate have a sense of what is essential and what is desirable.

Communication: Goal Setting

One of the most important factors in employment success is understanding what is expected of you and where you should be focusing your time and efforts. When factors are defined, it is easier for the new employee to be proactive in order to achieve success in that position. In other words, you and the new employee will both have a clearer understanding of what is expected or what the goals are that should be obtained.

Using the job description as a guide, you and your new hire can review the words in the description and set performance goals against them. This becomes a common communication tool that will benefit both of you and will help to avoid some misunderstanding in the future.

Some job descriptions will include percentages or weights to define the importance of one factor or task over another. That is a very effective way of helping the new employee to judge where to focus and spend the majority of his or her time.

Introduction

The job description can be utilized as a benchmark for determining whether the job is being performed according to expectations or whether goals are being exceeded. It can also help to measure problems and find out where performance is falling short of standards set. Finally, it can be used as a performance improvement tool to bring the employee up to performance expectations.

Performance Standards and Benchmarks

Once the employee is hired, the job description can become an aide for setting goals and expectations to measure performance. Tracking the performance on a regular basis will allow you to motivate and coach an employee who may not have begun the job on the strongest note but whom you feel has what it takes to succeed, if given guidance and encouragement.

A performance improvement plan, along with the job description, can be used either to save the job or to end the job of an employee who is not performing up to expectations. When the time comes to measure performance, it will be clear where the employee is not performing to expectations or to set standards.

A well-written job description can be the building block for better communications, better performance, and ultimately better success for all.

Finding the Best Candidate for the Job

The universal source of finding new employees today is through postings on the Internet. Use of this medium has increased the need for clear communications regarding the expectations and requirements of the job. An effort needs to be made to have the job sound interesting, as your company is competing for the same talent worldwide. A well-written job description is not only necessary but essential. When a job posting or ad reaches across the nation or the world, language must be clear, to describe what is expected, including the requirements, duties, responsibilities, and needs of this position.

Samples of job descriptions in *Perfect Phrases for Writing Job Descriptions* will give you a good idea of what constitutes a good job description. With this in hand, you will have the basic structure for building the "perfect job description."

Perfect Phrases™ for Writing Job Descriptions

Part One

The Job Analysis

The job description is the basic foundation for the hiring process.

Written correctly with some thought behind the process, the job description can serve many purposes in the hiring of the right person for the job, improve communication with the person once he or she is hired, and can even play a role in the success of a new hire.

Using a well-written job description to proceed through the hiring process can save both time and money. But the key benefit to be reaped from this document is to improve communication.

Communication is the basis for almost all interaction between people. And, it is the area that causes the most problems. Miscommunication and misunderstanding have been a major cause of problems since one person started talking to another. Sometimes we have a clear understanding of what we want and expect, but unless the person who you are communicating with has that same understanding, there is a breakdown in communication.

The job description can be used as a tool to try to avoid such miscommunication and breakdowns in understanding what one person wants and needs. Mainly what needs to be clear is what you want from the employee and how the employee understands what is important to you.

A job description needs to have multiple dimensions. It has to have a broad base of information that can be built upon and expanded as needed. At the same time it needs to be very specific in defining measurable objectives.

Writing the description and using a combination of the broad and the specific will have a tremendous impact on your selection process, your process of elimination, and your goal-setting process in the planning of the objectives for the new hire.

Because that description can be such a valuable communication tool, it would seem to be obvious that quality time and thought ought to be spent in the creation of the description. The reality, however, is that the up-front work of writing the job description is usually done in a very haphazard manner, if it is done at all. Many a job description is thrown together by adopting one that has been used previously or by taking one from some other source or another company's posting. With a little copying and pasting you have a job description. And more than likely it will be a very inadequate one. Certainly it won't be one that will be the basis of communication and goal setting between you and your new employee.

This casual approach to writing the job description is a formula for failure both in the hiring process and in the communications that will follow the hiring when it comes time to set the expectations and goals of the job.

On the other hand, if it is done correctly, the job description will be a wonderful segue to open up and to improve communications. Future goals and performance benchmarks can be discussed using a well-written job description. In fact, the job description becomes an agreement of sorts between the supervisor and the new hire to define performance goals and to set expectations.

A well-written job description will serve multiple purposes that will reap rewards before and after the hire—if done correctly.

Quality Time Spent Up-Front

In the following chapters you will find several examples and formulas to guide you through the process of analyzing and writing a quality job description. Taking time to think through the purpose of hiring a new person will allow you to analyze the necessity of this position in the bigger scheme of things.

You will be able to define the requirements, the experiences, the skills, the qualities, and the traits that you are seeking in a new hire to fill your open position. You will also produce a tool to assist you in your decision making and choice of the best candidate for the job.

You will only find what you are looking for if you have determined what it is you need and are seeking.

Chapter 1

A Well-Defined Job Description

The first and foremost use of the job description will be to locate qualified candidates for an open position. By creating your *ideal candidate* description you will stand a much better chance of finding the person whom you are seeking.

Ask yourself: "What would be my ideal situation to be solved by finding the right person?"

Begin to think of this description as your *wish list*.

Let's start with some basic questions to ask yourself:

"Why is it necessary to fill this position—at this time?"
"Could the responsibilities of this job be assigned to another employee?"
"What do I hope to accomplish by hiring a new person?"

This line of thinking and these questions should be your first step to be sure that you can justify the hiring of this person. Once you have justified the need for the hire, you can progress to the next step: to determine the experiences, qualifications, and skills that are necessary for a person to succeed in this position.

Notice the phrase "to succeed" is used rather than "to fill" this position. One of the biggest mistakes in hiring is to choose someone who can "fill" the position without the thought of long-term success. Depending on the job market and the economy, you will sometimes have few candidates to choose from and therefore settle for 80 percent of your "wish list."

In a "buyer's market" when you have numerous candidates to choose between, you can not only search for 100 percent of your desired qualities and experiences but also seek "added value."

Added value are skills or abilities that are above and beyond what is essential or even nonessential for the job. They are skills, traits, and experiences that would be a plus in this position. An example would be a person who is able to communicate in sign language or who is bilingual. These are not required skills to perform the job but would be something added that you could offer your customers who have special needs if someone brought those skills to the position.

The next set of questions to ask yourself is about the value of importance:

When weighing the value of what is important to the success of the business, what extra services could I offer if the person I hired had more than the required skills?

What could this person bring in addition to the basic requirements that would add value to the position?

How can these skills or abilities add value to the business or give additional service to our customers?

What new service could be added as a result of hiring a person with extra skills?

The Job Analysis

When all candidates appear equal in terms of experience and knowledge, it is sometimes the added value that will be the tiebreaker and determine the best candidate for the job. In other words, this would be a bargain or good deal to get more than you wished for in a candidate.

Here are some examples of added-value statements on a job description:

Excellent English language skills required—both written and spoken. Any knowledge of other Asian languages will be a big plus.

Financial services industry experiences a plus.

Call center experience preferred.

Proficient in Microsoft Office and Internet technologies. Excel and MS Project experience a plus.

Passion for assisting disadvantaged persons would be a great asset.

Second language skills and international business experience are desired.

Depending on the conditions of the employment market, you may be able to find someone who surpasses your needs and adds a special service. Doing so will take some creative thinking on your part as well as being open-minded about the person you hire. Just because there has been a certain type of person in the job before does not mean that you cannot reach out and make a paradigm shift in thinking about how the job could change. Change can be threatening when you are trying things that are not the "norm." But you will always get the same results if you continue to do things in the same manner.

Management and Executives

The qualifications and experiences you require will be affected by not only supply and demand but also the level of responsibility the new hire will have or need to have. Your qualifying questions will be dramatically different if you are writing a job description for a manager or executive versus writing a description for the position of, say, a mail clerk.

Writing a job description for managers and executives will require more details about the responsibilities of the job and the impact the decisions make on the bigger picture. The achievements, or the lack of achievement, of an executive may play a significant role on the success or failure of a department or a company.

Descriptions for these positions will require a definition of the culture and goals of the company as well as the expectations of the organization. A well-written job description at this level will define how this position will fit into the bigger picture. The job description will serve as a tool to set measurable goals to determine success.

Executive or management job descriptions will have more detail about the bottom line or impact of their decisions:

- Manage multimillion-dollar glazing projects for Florida Glass. Manage all project managers as well as oversee all of production.

- Work with the Analytics and Product Marketing teams to define the right target segments based on the capacity and performance of the Telesales group.

- Communicate with regional staff about comparative shopping analyses, fast and slow selling classifications and styles, planning and adjusting stock levels, and customer requests.

- As a member of the Technology Outside Sales team, the regional sales manager for the Northeastern region executes the company sales strategy throughout an identified geographical region.

- Works with minimal supervision and is responsible to make an established range of decisions, escalating to manager when necessary and updates manager on a regular basis.

Chapter 2

Identifying the Key Factors of the Job

Determining the key factors of the position will be the most important step to complete before you can begin to identify the requirements needed to succeed.

This process will require more questioning regarding the need for this position and the prospective of this position in the larger scheme of the company's goals.

Here are key questions to ask:

1. What are the goals of the company? The department? The position?
2. How does this position support the goals?
3. What would you like to see happen as a result of hiring a new person?
4. What added value do you require this person to bring to the position?
5. What would you like to be able to say about this new hire one year from now?

By writing your answers out you can begin to observe details and objectives that you may not have observed before this exercise and that now can be used as a guide to define the responsibilities of the job.

Responsibilities of the Job

Identifying key factors will determine the focus of the skills you are seeking in a candidate and will define the questions you will ask in the interview.

The key factors of the job are the primary or essential responsibilities and duties of the job. In other words, they define the main role or purpose of the position. Identifying skills needed under each area of responsibility you will begin to see a pattern of skills that will be necessary to get the job done.

By narrowing the list down to six to eight key factors you will identify the skill areas. These factors are usually measurable objectives of the job and are typically written as incomplete sentences that are a series of tasks; for example:

- Manages customer service clientele.
- Maintains the Account Database by providing updates on a weekly basis.
- Reviews insurance benefits and patient requirements as applicable.

Typically, each factor will either start with a verb or contain a verb as an indicator of an action required.

To define the factors, begin to write out a list of what the main duties, areas of responsibilities, or tasks will be.

Examples

- **Leads** the development and elevation of direct leaders and staff through proactive coaching, mentoring, professional development, and feedback.

- **Oversees** operations, facility, grant-funded programs, grant reporting, and staff of 17.

- **Provides** balanced execution of operations and business leadership in defining strategies that contribute to supporting strategic planning.

- **Manages** inventory plans from investment through allocation execution, including ongoing assessments and updates, for multiple departments.

- **Recruits** and **supervises** interns and volunteers to conduct surveys and interview patients.

- **Trains** and **motivates** the sales team and **promotes** team culture and values.

- **Analyzes** and **prepares** forecasts to project long-term and immediate workforce demands.

- **Creates** forms and procedures for work packets to increase efficiency.

- **Directs** and **manages** a team of bank tellers; training and scheduling work schedules.

- **Creates** and **implements** effective in-house procedures.

- **Conducts** audits of financial dealings within the corporation.

- **Manages** confidential correspondence, scheduling, and meetings for key executive.

- **Plans** and **directs** all office management for the CEO as well as other key executives.
- **Handles** a wide variety of writing tasks, from routine to creative features.
- **Plays key role** in all phases of planning, preparation, and execution of Achievement Awards.
- **Solidifies** and **strengthens** relations with the public through positive initiatives.
- **Verifies** compliance to release specifications on all products prior to shipment.

Example

Marketing Manager

Market managers are responsible for the gross profit in assigned markets, and will own inventory, cost, pricing, and merchandising decisions for that market.

Responsibilities

1. Develops and maintains supplier relationships at the property and chain level through daily contact.

   Skills Required—Communication Skills—Interpersonal Sensitivity—Create Motivating Environment, Informing

2. Analyzes contracts and executes pricing.

   Skills Required—Business Savvy, Analytical Skills/Ability to Work with Numbers, Decision-Making, Strategic, Big Picture Perspective, Negotiation

3. Implements extranet rate and inventory revisions, ensures suppliers understand extranet, and increases supplier usage of extranet.

    Skills Required—Flexibility, Informing, Customer Focus, Motivate, Accountable

4. Conducts weekly competitive analysis for key markets, reports findings, and makes adjustments.

    Skills Required—Analytical Thinking, Big Picture Thinking, Development Orientation, Adaptable

5. Monitors, evaluates, and reports on individual accounts and markets progress toward achieving weekly, monthly, annual targets.

    Skills Required—Ability to Hold People Accountable, Analytical, Decision Maker, Goal-Oriented, Big Picture Perspective

6. Understand key market hard/soft periods, know destinations and trends, create and maintain event calendars for key market locations, and plan courses of action required to meet supply, demand, and necessary sales.

    Skills Required—Business Savvy, Visionary, Trend Knowledge, Organized, Planner, Implement Action

7. Execute annual contract negotiations.

    Skills Required—Leadership, Strategic, Communication, Deal Maker, Closer, Negotiation Skills

Suggested Key Factors

1. Communication—build relationships
2. Leadership—accountability—self and others
3. Analytical Thinking—analysis of data
4. Visionary—big picture thinking
5. Ability to Influence—motivate, sell, negotiate
6. Business Savvy—current trends

In this example you can see that "reading between the lines" is essential. What would it take to do the job? What key factors can be identified by listing the tasks of the job?

Once you have narrowed down the factors to a sizeable number, you can begin to plan how you will write your job description as well as the interview questions you will ask to obtain information about the person's performance and experience pertaining to these key factors.

Chapter 3

Identifying the Skills Required

Once you have written the key factors, you can identify what skill sets it would take to do this job. You can begin to think about and list the skills necessary or desirable to carry out these responsibilities of the position.

The skills required can be categorized as *essential* job functions. These are the "must haves." Or, they may also fall into the *nonessential* job functions category. These skills and traits may be desirable to have but are not necessary to perform the duties of the job. Determining what is essential and what is nonessential to performance of a position is becoming a crucial factor in compliance with the Americans with Disabilities Act.

Essential Skills (Critical Skills)

When you have identified the purpose of the position, some critical skills that are absolutely required in order to succeed in a particular job will become clear. The number of critical skills should be approximately seven to nine, and can be labeled "must haves." These are the specifics of the position. If you do not include these in your job description, you will miss the mark in getting the desired candidates for your pool of potential employees.

Examples

Responsible for managing a detailed implementation project plan throughout the initial launch of the program.

Detailed project management and maintenance of ongoing operational initiatives required.

Responsible for analyzing and meeting required performance benchmarks.

Provide daily guidance and leadership to the managers, and other team members dedicated to the program.

Skills Required

Project Management, Leadership, Team Development, Client Rapport, Analytical Skills, Follow-Through, Big Picture Perspective

A minimum of five years in a supervisory position in a not-for-profit. Experience in budget management.

Program development experience.

Skills Required

Supervisory Experience, Industry Savvy, Budget/Accounting/ Finance Knowledge/Experience, Writing/Communication Skills, Organizational Skills

*As a core member of both the North America operating
leadership and a senior member of the global management
team of the Chief Information Officer (CIO), this executive is
expected to play an integral role in creating and
implementing business vision through the aggressive
utilization of information technologies (IT) and innovation.*

Skills Required

Leadership, Driving Results, Strategizing, Communication,
Global Management Experience, Critical and Creative Thinking,
Vision, IT Savvy

Example of Industry-Driven Knowledge: Highly Critical Skills

- Familiarity with developing software for resource-constrained embedded systems, especially Linux operating systems.
- Experience implementing Internet protocols.
- Experience implementing physical interfaces or drivers for Ethernet, USB [Universal Serial Bus], object-oriented analysis, and design.
- Secret security clearance.

Nonessential Duties (Secondary Skills)

Nonessential duties could be called peripheral, incidental, or
minimal parts of the job. The majority of job descriptions do
not list nonessential duties.

Examples

- May perform basic duties in other areas of the department.
- Participate and attend staff training, programs, and other training sessions.
- When requested, performs weekly reports and account summary reports.
- Perform additional duties as directed or assigned.
- Sales experience within the telecommunications industry would be an advantage, but not essential.
- Familiarity with culture, customs, and traditions helpful.
- Active affiliation with appropriate networks, organizations, and community involvement preferred.
- One to two years' work experience, preferred.
- Advanced supply chain experience recommended.
- Other duties as assigned.

Essential Duties and the Americans with Disabilities Act

The Americans with Disabilities Act 1990 (ADA) requires employers to consider the essential duties of a job in evaluations and applicant's qualifications. An essential duty is any task that is a basic, necessary, and integral part of the job.

In addition, when considering essentiality, one must focus upon whether the duty is essential to this particular job and not to the department as a whole.

Questions to clarify essential duties:

1. Are the duties required to be performed on a regular basis? If a duty is rarely performed, it may not be essential.
2. Is the duty highly specialized? The need for special expertise is an indication of an essential duty.

Questions to clarify nonessential duties:

1. Would removing the duty fundamentally change the job? If not, the duty is nonessential.
2. Are there other employees available to perform the duty? If it is feasible to redistribute the work, the duty may be nonessential.

Three Categories of Skills

In addition to the essential and nonessential classification of skills, we can place skills in three categories that will define the importance of the skill set. These three categories are another method of defining what is most important in the job match. They can sometimes make the difference between two or more equally qualified persons for the same job and how you decide on one person over another.

The three categories of skills are knowledge-based skills, transferable or general skills, and personal traits.

Knowledge-Based Skills

Knowledge-based skills may account for as much as 50 percent or more of the essential job functions—for example, to be technically savvy, to have a specific background, and to have special knowledge or certain degrees or to speak a foreign language.

Often these skills are the main focus of the job description, and the decision to hire is made solely on the candidate's fulfillment of these requirements. That approach is a mistake for many reasons. The new hire may be technically qualified but may not possess the other traits necessary to fit into the organization and the culture. That limitation will affect not only the department or organization but also the tenure of the employee, who is not a good fit for the environment.

Knowledge-based skills are skills learned through experience or education:

> Computer Programs/Languages; Graphics; Languages; Writing Skills; Training Skills; Management Experience; Sciences: e.g., Chemistry and Biology; Coaching Skills; Sales Experience; Leadership Training; Project Management; Operations; Marketing; Event Planning; Policy Development; Legal Expertise; Strategic Planning; Liaison; Mediator; Product Management; Research Skills; Business Acumen; Mechanically Adept

Transferable or General Skills

Transferable skills or general skills are not necessarily taught in any classroom. They are learned skills through maturity, development, and experience.

These can be the skills that set one candidate apart from the others. These skills are often considered as "nonessential" or softer skills. This is an unfortunate thinking, because when examined a little closer, transferable skills can be considered "added-value" and can also be essential to the success of the person's performance. In fact, most performance issues pertain to the "general" skills rather than the knowledge-based ones.

Transferable skills can be thought of as "portable" in the sense that you can take them with you to almost any job. They are *broad-based* and usually *learned* or *acquired through experience*:

> Communication; Listening; Decision Making; Judgment; Initiative; Planning; Organizing; Time Management; Leadership; Work Ethic; Interpersonal Skills; Common Sense; Social Skills; Creative Ideas; Sees Big Picture; Analytical; Accountable; Reliable; High Standards; Resourceful; Action-Oriented; Intuitive; Problem Solving; Good with Numbers; Gets Along Well; Articulate; Handy; Artistic; Envisioning

Personal Traits

Lastly, there are the personal traits that may be connected to a person's EQ, or "emotional quotient." These skills have been measured against the IQ, or Intelligence Quotient as being a very important factor in a person's ability to cope and get along with life issues.

Personal traits are the qualities that will determine a fit in the company, the department, or the position. Although these abilities are sometimes considered to be soft skills and nonessential to the job, they are often the ones that can affect the performance of a person and should not be taken lightly when seeking the ideal candidate for your situation.

Personal traits are attributes that define a person's *personality*:

Dependable; Strong; Team Player; Versatile; Patient; Friendly; Energetic; Formal; Loyal; Self-Confident; Dynamic; Practical; Sociable; Persuasive; Responsible; Sense of Humor; Cheerful; Good Attitude; Aggressive; Assertive; Determined; Honest; Humble; Productive; Conscientious; Curious; Enthusiastic, Precise; Detail-Oriented; Compassionate; Efficient; Emotional; Rigid; Open-Minded

Judging a Candidate Based on His or Her Skills

Any time you are seeking the ideal person, all three categories should come into play. Judging a person solely on his or her knowledge-based skills may deal with the surface problem of getting the job done, but it is a wise hiring employer who looks beyond the knowledge-based skills to the other qualities the person has.

Here are some basic questions to ask during or after the interview:

■ Will this person fit into the organization?

The Job Analysis

- Are there red flags or patterns that you are picking up about this person's work history?
- Does this person know his or her area of expertise? Can this person communicate to others what he or she knows?

Chapter 4

Requirements of the Job

The requirements of the job are those qualities from your "wish list" that you would find desirable in your ideal candidate. Obviously, there will be some areas that are more subjective and flexible than others; for example, you may desire six years of industry experience but be willing to settle for four years of experience with some education or other job-related training.

On the other hand, the critical skill may be "hard and fast" and there may be no flexibility in order for the person to succeed in this job.

Examples of Requirements of the Job

- An undergraduate degree is required. A minimum of five years in a supervisory position in a not-for-profit.

- Able to use rigorous logic and methods to solve problems with effective solutions (Problem Solving & Decision Quality).

- Experience and success speaking in public, in front of customers, press, analysts, and company executives.
- Must have proven track record in product management and strategic thinking, working with fast-paced team of enterprise software developers.
- Effective team management experience/skills in a matrix and geographically dispersed international organization in a rapidly changing environment.
- Expert programmer in C/C++ and assembly language.
- Manage inventory plans from investment through allocation execution, including ongoing assessments and updates, for multiple departments.
- Ability to think objectively and interpret meaningful themes from quantitative and qualitative data (Analytic Skills).
- Perform contract and price negotiations, prepare the contractual documents, and close the sale with clients.

For the most part, these examples appear to be hard and fast and essential to the success of the job. In an employer's choice market, where there are more candidates than there are jobs, these essentials will be required ... and then some. In a market where there is a shortage of candidates or at least candidates from certain disciplines, these factors may become more flexible.

Here's an example of a requirement in an employer market with many candidates to choose from:

An undergraduate degree is required. A minimum of five years in a supervisory position in a not-for-profit.

The description in a market with fewer candidates to choose from might read:

An undergraduate degree with some supervisory experience desired. Not-for-profit experience highly desirable.

As in all commodities, supply and demand rules the accessibility. This rule reverts back to the writing of the job description that should be broad enough to be built upon, yet specific enough to define the job and to attract desirable candidates.

One way of defining an essential requirement of the job is to assign percentages to the importance of the responsibility.

Examples

- Perform contract and price negotiations, prepare the contractual documents, and close the sale with clients. (Importance—50 percent)
- Experience and success speaking in public, in front of customers, press, analysts, and company executives. (Importance—20 percent)

Other Skills, Abilities, and Requirements

This can be the "catch-all" category for anything else that seems important to the position but does not quite fit into the responsibilities or the requirements sections.

Examples

- The candidate should be able to work on his or her own without any supervision.
- Must be able to work evenings and weekends.
- Ability to maintain confidentiality.
- Passion for assisting a disadvantaged population.
- Successful candidates must be available to travel and work in excess of standard hours when necessary.
- High degree of self-motivation and the ability to work independently.
- Ability to work under pressure in a demanding environment.

Part Two

Writing the Job Description

Once you have justified the need for the position and identified the key factors as well as the skills required, you will have successfully laid the groundwork to pull all your information together. You will now have all the components necessary to begin the writing of a successful job description.

The "Who," "What," and "Why," of the Job Description

Some of the basic tools of good writing begin with these questions:

"Who?"

"What?"

"Why?"

When you have dealt with these three questions you will be able to write with a more focused emphasis as to why this position exists and what you will require from the person who fills this position.

Who?

Who will be a likely person to succeed in this position? What background and experience is necessary?

Examples

A seasoned professional, a new graduate, a results-driven leader, a competent support person, a top-notch executive, an analytical expert, the ultimate coordinator, a creative problem solver, an expeditor, a master planner, a decision maker, a team player

Seeking a seasoned professional to lead a team to the next level of marketing a new product.

This position is open to recent grads who are willing to become a member of a fast-paced environment.

This position requires a decision maker who can hit the ground running and deal with new and existing issues.

We are in need of the ultimate coordinator to push through a number of projects simultaneously.

This is a key position for a competent support person who will work with a diverse workforce at various levels.

What?

What personal qualities will be required to succeed in this position?

Examples

Extroverted, high energy, analytical thinker, decision maker, stable and steady, quiet and reflective, powerful,

confident, mature, composed, relentless, forward thinking, business savvy, objective, open-minded, honest,
forthright

*This is a high-stress-level position requiring stamina and high
energy to meet tight deadlines and handle demanding
customers.*

*We are seeking a visionary or forward thinker to strategically
plan and develop our mission over the next five years.*

*Confidentiality is an absolute must for this position. Seeking a
mature-minded individual who can assure confidence and
trust to our clients.*

*Analytical problem solver is needed to take raw data and
organize, analyze, and make recommendations.*

*This position requires a hard-driving person with business savvy
who has industry connections and knows the competition
and the trends of our products.*

Why?

Why do you need to hire a new person?

Examples

To improve customer relations, to motivate and manage staff, to be a visionary, to market a new product, to
analyze problems, to analyze marketing results,
to drive sales, to create and implement, to play an integral role in global relations, to be the arbitrator, to
be the negotiator, to lead the effort, to solve technical problems

Due to an extensive growth of our product line, we are in need of a savvy marketing person to benchmark and drive sales and take us to a new place in the industry.

Our company has undergone a global transformation and is seeking an executive to play an integral role in creating and implementing our business vision.

Seeking a leader to work with high-growth clients and other market leaders in industries such as retail, consumer products, financial services, insurance, and health sciences.

We are looking for a candidate with financial and business acumen to evaluate financial and business indicators and to translate data into actionable information to drive results.

As a product manager, you will lead the effort in delivering world-class products. You will conduct and utilize continuous competitive research. We are seeking an individual who will deliver products that win awards and generate high customer satisfaction ratings.

By satisfying the who, what, and why questions you will begin to determine the vocabulary and words that will enhance your job description to attract more interest by qualified job seekers.

"The better the match, the better the chances for employee satisfaction, the better the retention rate for your company."

Chapter 5

Bringing It All Together: Assembling the Parts

I f you followed along with the method, you are now ready for the next step in writing the perfect job description. It is now time to put all the pieces together in an organized manner into one document.

Styles: Formal or Informal?

The styles used in writing job descriptions may vary from very formal, with an impressive format on customized letterhead or logo, to a simple "fill in the blanks" type of format. The job and the candidate you are trying to attract may dictate the extent of the presentation.

Regardless of the format used, the content needs to contain standard information if it is to be well written. The mission of the job description is to give as much information to the job seeker as possible to seek a good match between what you are looking for and what the candidate is seeking.

A poorly written job description lacks important information and may only contain the bare facts, a quick summary of the job description, and some contact information.

Another example of an unsatisfactory job description that presents a poor image is when all the text is crammed together with no white space utilized; it is really nothing more than a list of tasks given in no particular order. These types of descriptions not only are difficult to read, they are boring as well.

Example of a Poorly Written Job Description

HR Director

The major areas directed are:

- Recruitment and staffing;
- Performance management and improvement systems;
- Organizational development;
- Employment and compliance to regulatory concerns;
- Employee orientation, development, and training;
- Policy development and documentation;
- Employee relations, union negotiations;
- Safety Committee facilitation, Quality Improvement and Disaster Committee member;
- Employee communication;
- Compensation and benefits administration;
- Employee safety, wellness, welfare, and health;
- Employee services and counseling.

Writing the Job Description

Primary Objectives

- Safety of the workforce.
- Development of a superior workforce.
- Development of the Human Resources department.
- Development of an employee-oriented culture that emphasizes quality care, continuous improvement, culture change in long-term care, customer service, and high performance.
- Personal ongoing development.

Essential Job Functions

- Oversees the implementation of Human Resources programs through Human Resources staff. Monitors administration to established standards and procedures. Identifies opportunities for improvement and resolves any discrepancies.
- Oversees and manages the work of reporting Human Resources staff. Encourages the ongoing development of Human Resources staff.
- Develops and monitors an annual budget that includes Human Resources services, employee recognition, and administration.
- Coordinates use of broker, insurance carriers, pension administrators, and other outside resources.
- Conducts a continuing study of all Human Resources policies, programs, and practices to keep management informed of new developments.

■ Leads the development of department goals, objectives, and systems.

■ Establishes departmental measurements that support the accomplishment of the Jewish Home strategic goals.

■ Prepares periodic reports for management, as necessary or requested, to track strategic goal accomplishment.

■ Participates in Department Head meetings and staff meetings and attends other meetings.

Example of Bringing Order to Chaos

By taking each category and assigning duties to each category, this same jumbled job description takes on a new dimension. It is very difficult for anyone to read a jumbled list of disjointed tasks and be attracted to the position from reading such a job description.

Taking the time to categorize tasks into specific areas of responsibility makes a huge difference in the comprehension of the job and what it entails.

Human Resources Management

Development of the Human Resources department: goals, objectives, and systems.

■ Develops and monitors an annual budget that includes Human Resources services, employee recognition, and administration. Responsible for preparing key HR-related statistical reports and other periodic reports for management, as necessary or requested, to track strategic goal accomplishment.

- Coordinates use of brokers, insurance carriers, pension administrators, and other outside resources.
- Participates in Department Head meetings and staff meetings and attends other meetings and seminars, monitoring HR-related issues.

Policies and Procedures

- Human Resources Director coordinates implementation of services, policies, and programs through Human Resources staff; reports to the administrator and serves on the Department Head team; and assists and advises department heads about Human Resources issues.
- Conducts a continuing study of all Human Resources policies, programs, and practices to keep management informed of new developments. Protects the interests of employees in accordance with policies and governmental laws and regulations.
- Leads compliance with all existing governmental and labor legal and government reporting requirements and is responsible for the preparation of information requested or required for compliance with laws. Approves all information submitted.
- Develops an employee-oriented culture that emphasizes quality care, continuous improvement, culture change in long-term care, customer service, and high performance.

Employee Relations

- Determines and recommends to senior management and/or department heads employee relations practices to promote a high level of employee morale and motivation.
- Responsible for performance management and improvement systems combined with employee services and counseling.
- Oversees the implementation of Human Resources programs through HR staff.
- Identifies opportunities for improvement and resolves any discrepancies.
- Creates, monitors, and advises managers in the progressive discipline system. Monitors implementation of performance improvement process with nonperforming employees.
- Reviews with and guides department heads about recommendations for employment terminations. Participates in investigations. Abides by zero tolerance for abuse and state and federal mandated laws.
- Conducts employee complaint investigations when they are brought forth. Reviews employee appeals through the complaint procedure. Participates with administrator in union-related grievances.

Recruitment and Staffing

- Establishes and leads the standard recruiting and hiring practices and procedures necessary to recruit and hire a superior workforce.

- Oversees pre-employment screening, pre-employment physical, and tuberculosis (TB) testing requirements, and mandated background checks.

Compensation/Benefits Administration

- Establishes wage and salary structure, leads competitive market research to pay practices and pay bands that help recruit and retain superior staff.
- Comonitors with Controller all pay practices and systems for effectiveness and cost containment.
- Works with the Chief Financial Officer, obtains cost-effective employee benefits, monitors national benefits environment for options and cost savings.

Training and Development

- Defines all Human Resources training programs. Provides necessary education and materials to department heads, managers, and employees, including workshops, manuals, employee handbooks, and standardized reports.
- Establishes an in-house employee training system: training needs assessment, new employee orientation, management development, cross-training, and transfer training.

Safety

- Safety Committee facilitation, Quality Improvement and Disaster Committee member;

■ Leads the implementation of safety and health programs. Monitors the tracking of required date for OSHA [Occupational Safety and Health Administration].

When the information is presented in a chaotic manner, the candidate must "read between the lines" and can sometimes overlook a very good opportunity because of a lack of information.

The Key Parts of the Job Description

Not all job descriptions are created equal, and some will have company information about the culture and purpose of the work the company performs. There are no hard or fast rules about how much information should be given about the company. Nevertheless, if the purpose of the job description is to improve communications, it would seem to be a good idea to include as much information as possible to attract the candidate and to avoid a misunderstanding of what the company does and what the mission of the company is.

Company Information: Culture, Mission, History

Here are some examples of company information, including history, product definition, goals, values, and missions:

The Charity Company has provided voluntary helping programs since 1949. Its Family Resource Center was established to assist central city residents with support and education in parenting skills, youth and adult support groups, and life-skills training.

Headquartered in Pleasantville, AnyCompany employs more than 20,000 employees and operates 10 major manufacturing plants. AnyCompany designs, manufactures, and sells products to fit any vehicle, including airplanes, automobiles, bicycles, farm equipment, heavy-duty trucks, and motorcycles.

RJF Corporation is a leading provider of security solutions that identify and deliver award-winning, quality products to individual households, businesses, and corporations. Our products are in compliance with audit controls by all government agencies.

View Point products help customers understand what data risks they have, and which actions to take to protect that data. These products combine View Point's real-time event analysis and monitoring products. The result is a complete view of user activity to prevent fraud or data theft.

Lucky is one of America's largest parking operators, managing more than 600 businesses in 20 states across the United States. We currently employ over 3,000 employees. Our mission is to continually develop and expand our company and our people. We believe in equal opportunity for all.

The Justification for This Position: The Why

The justification usually defines the reason the position exists and the expectations of the overall job.

Examples

Intelligent Group is in the process of change, and we are looking for someone to write and maintain new diagnostics for our designs. We are seeking a Senior Network Software Engineer to develop communication and wireless products. This position is responsible for the design, development, and maintenance of our software for wireless products.

The Amber Company is opening a new division in YellowVille, and is seeking an HR Director to start up our Human Resources Department. At Amber, we value talented, dedicated employees and consider them to be the most important element in achieving and maintaining our excellent standards. We provide an enjoyable and satisfying work environment.

This is a new position for a Department Coordinator who will have front-line responsibility for all contact prior to, during, and at the conclusion of the patient's course of care. This is a key position, and the coordinator will be involved in the scheduling of patient support and the follow-up during the testing phase and patient education.

We have recently merged forces with an international company and are seeking a qualified data entry and customer service–oriented individual to become a Data Center Coordinator. In this position the Data Entry representatives will be responsible for all communication with our offshore affiliate and will be held responsible for problem solving that may include traveling 25 percent of the time to a foreign country.

Amazing Corporation is looking for a product marketing manager to launch 1.0 version of our new products. This person will manage product life cycle and product definition of the product suite and must enjoy working with engineering, sales, press, analysts, and of course customers to bring cutting-edge products to market.

Desirable Personality Traits

This is a somewhat subjective category. Some job descriptions will move from the overview into the responsibility of the job, and some will have an introduction paragraph describing the person they are seeking.

By including personality traits you are giving the readers a better idea of what to expect and whether they are a good fit for the culture of the company as much as for the job.

Here are some examples of descriptions of personal characteristics that describe what characteristics are desirable or necessary to perform the position:

Our ideal candidate will thrive in a challenging and structured environment. This person will have a proactive approach to problem identification and resolutions.

Seeking a bright, very organized, detail-oriented, confident and efficient Office Manager with great people-skills and a "can-do" attitude.

Flexibility and openness to new thinking is a must in this position. This person must be able to survive in a fast-paced retail environment. You will require a results-oriented mindset.

This position requires exceptional ability to communicate and work with a wide variety of customers. We are looking for someone with an appreciation and respect for the diversity of all individuals in the workplace.

We need a positive and caring person to manage our team and live by our mission of high standards and a superior work ethic. He or she must be able to maintain confidentiality of pertinent information.

"The more objective your process is, the less discriminatory your decision will be."

Key Factors for the Job: Essential Duties

These factors will be a composite or list of responsibilities of the job on a day-to-day and long-term basis.

Examples

Maintains all data changes and keeps records of work completed in the appropriate manner consistent with the policies and procedures.

Performs outbound calling to schedule delivery of testing unit. Reviews insurance benefits and patient requirements that are applicable.

Responsible for the business, management, operation, financial, and strategic performance of product lines.

Collaborates with other marketing leaders to develop an overall marketing and promotional strategy.

Train, coach, and provide direction to supervisory staff on basic skills of supervision and conducting performance appraisals.

These are the core duties of the job and should be written as clear, declarative sentences usually beginning with a verb.

Requirements

Many job descriptions put more emphasis on what the candidate should bring to the table than they do in telling the candidate what is expected. But you can improve the job description and in the process can also have better communications that attract the right candidates.

Here are some examples of focused requirements statements:

B.S. degree in Pharmacy or Health Sciences resulting in the ability to become an Authorized User.

A bachelor's degree required, and a Masters of Business Administration preferred.

Approximately 3 to 4 years of relevant work experience.

At least 5 years of progressively responsible experience in project management or related area.

Proficiency in PC applications, including Microsoft Word and Excel, and contact management software.

Writing the Job Description and Starting from Scratch for a New Position

It is always more challenging to write from scratch, beginning with a blank piece of paper or a blank screen, than it is to edit a previously written job description. That is the main reason that job descriptions tend to get used over and over again. It's very easy and convenient to copy and paste and put very little time or thought into the importance of the document.

The temptation to use a previously written job description is strong because of time constraints, but the benefits of starting from scratch, or at least analyzing a description that has been used before, will, in the long run, be time well spent.

Taking the time to analyze the job and to write a new version of the expectations of the job will ensure that you are not repeating behaviors and expectations that may not have been effective in the past or that may be outdated or inefficient because of new technology.

Although this task may seem like a daunting one, it will move quickly if you take the time to answer the questions asked previously and think through the who, what, and why reasons for your decision to seek out a new employee.

As you move through the process and see your job description develop into a clearer picture with a direction for you to follow, you will be glad that you took the time to analyze before creating. By doing the groundwork you are well on your way to creating a successful job description.

Using a Previously Written Job Description for a Job Replacement

If you choose to use a job description that has been around for a while or taken from some other source, you risk skipping some important steps, which may cost you down the line. Nevertheless, there are instances when using a formerly used job description may be useful and save time.

When a previously written job description is used as a guide to determine what has worked or not worked in the past it can be very useful. This process allows you to determine what you would like to change about the position and the responsibilities or requirements of the job. Perhaps this is the time to upgrade the position. Or, possibly the position needs to be combined with another job by adding new dimensions.

Thinking "out of the box" can result in more efficient use of time and the labor force. By continuing to think that the job is the same and shouldn't be changed you may be missing an opportunity to save time, money, or head count.

By asking the same questions used to determine the need for the position in the previous chapter you can accept or reject all or parts of the job description as previously written.

You can also look at this job description to answer the following questions:

"What would you like more of?"

or

"What would you like less of?"

In other words, if the position has been responsible for a particular task that has taken a great deal of time but now could be replaced with an automated system or a new technology, you might consider changing the expectations of the job and replacing them with new requirements or new skill sets.

In a world of work where we think in terms of "lean and mean" and more efficiency, it may be time to combine duties into two or three other positions and possibly eliminate head count. Think of this effort as a "cleaning out" or "rearranging" process.

When you feel good about the position you are about to recruit for, you will have a better feeling for who will be the best candidate to fill this position.

By starting each new employee with realistic expectations and goals for the position you will open communications about the goals of the job from the beginning of the relationship.

It is always easier to succeed if you know what is expected of you.

Many employees begin their jobs not knowing the expectations or goals due to a lack of communication. As a result, they sometimes flounder for the first few months trying to determine if their performance is meeting standards.

A percentage of these employees will fail if they are left on their own to figure out the way. By stepping in from the beginning as their motivator and clearly communicating with them about the role and expectations of the job you will have a far better chance of retaining this employee as a success story rather than a failure.

> "The definition of insanity is doing the same thing over and over and expecting different results."
>
> —Albert Einstein

Attract the Candidates; Don't Discourage Them

Your goal is to create a job description that will define the challenges of the position and not just the tasks that will be performed. If you just list the tasks, not only will the job seeker lose out by becoming discouraged and disinterested and failing to apply for the job, but you will also lose out as the employer who fails to attract and get the best candidates. Any marketing person knows that the way you write a particular statement can have a tremendous effect on the person you are trying to influence and sell to (for the employers, that would be the job candidate).

Example of a statement lacking challenge

- Will lead development of direct leaders and staff.

Example of challenging statement

- Continually lead the development and elevation of direct leaders and staff through proactive coaching, mentoring, professional development, and feedback.

It is obvious that the first statement lacks passion and energy. When your job description lacks enthusiasm about the job it also lacks the screening mechanism that will weed out the wrong types of people from the right type of person. In this case, the challenging statement will help you locate the more *proactive* people and weed out the *reactive* people. You are not just looking for someone to lead development, you are seeking a leader who can elevate and motivate the team by using coaching and mentoring as a tool.

The Basics

The basics of a job description should include the following:

- **A Company Overview (optional, but encouraged)—** What the company does or the mission statement

Examples

ABC is one of North America's largest [type of company], managing more than [number of employees]. ABC's mission is to continually develop and expand our company and our people.

Founded in 1990, our company designs and develops technology for delivery into a wide variety of global market segments.

XYZ is among the most ambitious companies you will ever encounter. Through our businesses, we're working to make the newest technology perform better for more people. We think our system is more efficient than any other software that is available today.

- **The Industry**—The type of work done by the company (e.g., manufactures, consults, audits); The field of business (e.g., banking, pharmaceutical, finance, legal)
- **The Location of the Position or Corporate Location**— Geographic proximity; Address
- **The Title of the Job**—This will vary from company to company and position to position
- Administration Assistant, Secretary, Department Coordinator, Office Manager
- **Key Factor: Characteristics Description**—Overview of the expectations of the position; The more detail given, the more likely you are to find the right person.

Example:

We are seeking a [title] to fill [type of role] in our [name of department]. This position is responsible for [duties] to ensure [desired performance objectives or outcomes]. This role serves as the key point of contact for both internal and external clients regarding [responsibilities].

Our ideal candidate will [list expectations].

Looking for a [type of person] to launch [name of product set] and then guide and manage the growth of this product set going forward.

This person will manage [people or team].

Must enjoy working with [types of people with whom the candidate will be working]. This candidate will be able to do [responsibilities and tasks].

In this position you will be directly responsible for maintaining [responsibilities].

This function will involve sales to new customers, additional sales to existing customers, and retaining existing customers through training and providing customer service with added value to customer's services. You will create, and develop [types of] presentations to [group being presented to] at events/conferences.

■ **Primary Responsibilities—**

  ■ Responsible for ...

  ■ Manages ...

  ■ Ensures ...

  ■ Able to ...

  ■ Take charge ...

  ■ Maintains ...

  ■ Provides ...

- **Requirements—**
  - Education ...
  - Knowledge ...
  - Experience ...

More Information Encourages More Trust

Because there are so many scams on the Internet regarding jobs that do not exist and false advertising, some job searchers have become suspicious about postings from smaller, unknown companies. It is important to be sure that you give adequate information on the job description so that the searcher can find information to verify your business claims.

Some job descriptions list benefits and compensation information. How this information is handled is a policy issue with each company. Supplying this information will not be necessary until the recruiting process has begun.

Example of a Well-Written Job Description

(This is a composite job description, for format purposes only.)

Company Information: Culture, Mission, and History

Good Job Network is an innovative industry leader distinguished by its pioneering spirit. Ever since our establishment in 1980, we've been the ideal workplace for people with adventurous spirit and creativity, who are smart risk takers and aggressive winners—all those for whom the status quo just isn't enough. Our Fortune 250 company continues to define the curve in television entertainment.

The Justification for This Position: The Why

We are always improving and extending our products and delivering greater value to people, including our workforce of 25,000 plus. Come explore the big picture with us!

Desirable Personality Traits

If you have the drive and desire to be a part of the best network, this is the place to be. We offer individualized career paths and exceptional earning potential.

Key Factors for the Job: Essential Duties

The Inventory Specialist manages the flow of material and equipment (satellite dishes, our award-winning receivers and associated hardware) in and out of the warehouse, supporting both our internal and external customers.

- Reviews upcoming satellite installations and pulls necessary hardware and equipment for satellite installers
- Receives returned equipment from satellite installers and inventories and sorts to be shipped for refurbishment
- Receives and verifies new inventory and adds the inventory to the warehouse

- Compiles and maintains records of quantity, type, and value material, equipment, merchandise, and/or supplies stocked in establishment and/or items to be returned
- Maintains an accurate inventory count of all products warehoused on a daily, weekly, and/or monthly format as required
- Verifies, formats, and prints reports
- Maintains an accurate inventory count of items ready to issue and ready to return to vendor by performing daily physical counts and automated inventory transactions and adjustments as necessary
- Formats and provides daily and weekly inventory status reports, as appropriate
- Assists supervisor with all inventory replenishment reports and inventory interactions with other departments and vendors

Requirements: Qualifications

Education

High school diploma or GED [General Educational Development certification] and 2 years of work experience are preferred. A background check and drug test will be preformed as part of pre-employment.

Skills and Qualifications

- Must be willing to work flexible hours; these positions will work evening hours (4–12 p.m.) and weekends.

- Ability to read and comprehend simple instructions, short correspondence, and memos
- Must also be able to write simple correspondence and effectively present information in one-on-one and small group situations to customers, clients, and other employees of the organization

Special Requirements
Physical Demands

- Employees must frequently lift and/or move up to 75 pounds
- May occasionally be required to lift up to 125 pounds
- Employees must be able to safely operate warehouse equipment (pallet jack, Big Joe, and/or a forklift)
- Frequent bending, lifting, twisting, and grasping

Benefits Offered

- Medical, Health Savings Account, dental and vision insurance
- Flexible spending options and Employee Assistance Plan
- 401(k) and Employee Stock Purchase Plan
- Tuition reimbursement
- Employee Referral Program

- Opportunity for a level of responsibility that could take years to reach in other companies

Additional Information

Good Job is a drug-free workplace; we are an equal opportunity employer.

Example of a Well-Written Job Description

(No company information is given, only the bare facts.)

Inventory Planner Position

Description

- The Inventory Planner supports Inventory Management by creating and managing sales and inventory plans from investment through allocation at the product/category/item level. The Inventory Planner is responsible for developing the assortment, demand, and inventory plans to achieve divisional financial plans.

- Manage an Inventory Planner Analyst by creating a collaborative, innovative, and results-oriented environment

- Balance workload priorities to ensure successful execution of inventory management

- Support the career development and skill development of Inventory Planner Analyst to ensure job satisfaction, retention, and future talent development

- Develop department- and class-level plans that support division strategy

- Develop preseason style plans and recommend investment quantities

- Develop department level allocation strategies

- Manage inventory plans from investment through allocation execution, including ongoing assessments and updates, for multiple departments

- Forecast in-season sales and inventory and develop risk mitigation strategies as needed

- Manage the reconciliation of class-to-department bottom-up plans

- Complete open-to-buy activities at department level

- Monitor progress of product receipts "end to end," from product booking to in-store, and ensure that purchase quantities align with plans and other systems

- Strategize, recommend, and execute in-season pricing strategies at style level

- Implement and execute advance supply chain techniques and approaches

Qualifications

- Analytic Skills: Ability to think objectively and interpret meaningful themes from quantitative and qualitative data

- Financial and Business Acumen: Ability to evaluate financial and business indicators and translate data into actionable information to drive results; proficiency in retail math

- Problem Solving and Decision Quality: Able to use rigorous logic and methods to solve problems with effective solutions

- Systems and Tools Acumen: Proficiency in Microsoft Excel, and aptitude to learn technical applications quickly
- Able to build constructive and effective relationships with a broad and diverse group of business partners
- Possess strong organizational and time management skills
- Demonstrate strong listening, written, and oral communication skills
- Bachelor's degree or equivalent experience
- 1–2 years' work experience preferred
- Advanced supply chain experience recommended

Primary Location

US-CA-SAN FRANCISCO

Employment Status

Full-time

Other Locations

Working Safely is a Condition of Employment at _____. An Affirmative Action Employer M/F/D/V [Male/Female/Disabled/Veteran].

Top Ten Benefits from Writing a Good Job Description

1. It is the foundation for the job hiring.

2. It can help you justify the position and what you want to accomplish by hiring this person.

3. It can define what you want in a new hire.

4. It is your best recruiting tool.

5. It can attract the best candidates, if it is well written and looks interesting.

6. It can act as a filtering device to help you stay focused on what it will take for the new hire to be successful in this position.

7. It will help you develop more focused interview questions to screen out the "real" answers.

8. It can improve communications once the new hire begins the job.

9. It will make performance issues easier to discuss, because you will have benchmarks to guide you and the new hire.

10. It will help you find the right fit with a new hire who will be satisfied with the job and stay longer—improving your retention rate.

Part Three

Quick Phrases References

The purpose of this section is to provide phrases to assist you in the writing of your job description. By using some of these phrases you will be able to expedite the writing process. These phrases will cover a range of positions from clerical and administrative to the more senior management positions.

This is a random sampling of phrases to use in the "duties portion" of your job description. By selecting from the various duties you will be able to customize the phrases you want to use when writing your job description.

Chapter 6

Clerical to Management Positions*

The following are descriptions of a number of positions from clerical to management. Titles may vary from company to company, but the duties or responsibilities will fall into similar categories.

The job descriptions in this category are **General Office and Clerical** positions. The titles included are: **Office Clerk, Retail Sales Clerk, Insurance Clerk. Administrative Assistant, Customer Service Representative**. Alternative titles are also listed.

---

*Information has been obtained from the following sources: *Dictionary of Occupational Titles*, Fourth Edition, Revised 1991; U.S. Department of Labor; O*NET Online; Monster.com; Salary.com.

Definition of Office Clerk

Performs a variety of duties. Responsibilities may vary and
may include a wide range of tasks: everything from
receptionist answering phones to scheduling of
calendars and assisting with general office tasks, such as
filing and opening mail.

May have a broader scope of responsibility—e.g., making
travel arrangements and booking conference rooms—or
have a specific area of responsibility, such as working
with vendors or supply inventory control.

Alternative Job Titles

Receptionist, Clerk, Secretary, Office Assistant, Office Clerk,
Office Coordinator

Phrases for Duties

■ Responsible for greeting visitors and making them and
vendors feel welcome. Assures that proper sign-in
procedures are followed and security precautions taken.

■ Answers the phones in an amiable and professional
manner. Answers any questions that are within the area
of the position's responsibility or refers the call to a
preassigned person to give advice or answer questions.

■ Serves as the general contact with employees, customers,
and other visitors to answer questions, give information,
or direct problems to the appropriate person.

- Operates any office machines within area of responsibility and reports any breakdowns or problems to the appropriate person or company.

- May file records or do miscellaneous paperwork as needed for individuals or departments.

- May be responsible for opening and sorting mail and delivering it to the appropriate person, or arrange for delivery by a mail carrier.

Retail Salesclerk

Definition of Retail Salesclerk

Works with a line of products ranging from basic consumer goods to apparel and larger merchandise such as appliances, furniture, and cars.

Works directly with the customer and assists whenever possible to fill the order and sell the merchandise or service.

Receives payment and follows procedures to ensure that the funds are handled according to the processing rules.

Receives and arranges orders for repairs, rentals, and services.

Explains available options, various charges, and policy on refunds to customers.

Assists with the display or upkeep of the merchandise and department to maintain an inviting environment.

Alternative Job Titles

Sales Associate, Sales Consultant, Salesperson, Customer Service Representative

Phrases for Duties

- Responsible for greeting customers and making them feel welcome; offering to assist them in any way possible.
- Uses sales techniques to sell merchandise to customers who have a need or are interested in further information.

- Provides excellent customer service to ensure that customers make return visits. Answers questions regarding store policies, procedures, merchandise, and return of merchandise.

- Works within policy guidelines and uses judgment within the authority of the position.

- Works with cash payments, checks, and credit cards and performs procedures for handling them. Calculates prices and taxes as appropriate to the sale.

- Is resourceful and helpful in providing customers with information, including other sources outside the company where the customer can go if sale merchandise is not available.

- Handles any problems with customers independently. Uses judgment when to refer the issue to the manager. Is aware of any security issues or problems, and deals with them appropriately.

- Uses good judgment when dealing with difficult situations; knowing when to call for help within or outside the department or store. Reports any problems of a suspicious or uncontrollable nature to security or law enforcement for assistance.

- Is familiar with safety policies and procedures and how to handle emergency situations of any type.

- Continues to keep abreast of current sales and promotions. Is knowledgeable about any coupons or discounts being offered. Processes discount, if valid and appropriate within company policy.

Insurance Claims Representative

Definition of Insurance Claims Representative

Provides service to insured members and potential customers and obtains information on their needs for policies that are offered. Uses tact and diplomacy in interviewing the customers regarding any situations that have occurred that may involve loss of life or property.

Responsible for paperwork and forms to settle the claims, deny the claims, or work with representatives from other insurance carriers to settle the claims.

Alternative Job Titles

Claims Adjuster, Claims Service Representative, Insurance Specialist

Phrases for Duties

- Interacts with members or customers, ensuring that their needs are met regarding purchase of policies for life, home, or automobile or any other services offered.

- Prepares any documentation and process verification as necessary for the purchase of new policies.

- Makes judgment calls to deny, settle, or authorize payments for routine claims. Arranges for payment or schedules payments according to the procedures defined by company policy.

- Obtains information from customers regarding any loss or mishaps after the purchase of the policy. Use judgment and diplomacy when dealing with customers who have endured a tragedy or loss.

- Follows all procedures to file claims and provide services as defined by company policy.

- Responsible for negotiation and settlement of loss, including fees, liens, and storage fees.

- Ensures customers that difficult situations will be handled in an efficient manner. Directs problems to the next level of management when necessary.

- Provides a list of resources to the customers in accordance with company practices and policies.

- Explains to customers any special circumstances or procedures that will affect a claim and future payment.

- Performs general office duties: filling out paperwork and forms, organizing claim reports, and filing records or entering them into database.

Definition of Administrative Assistant

General office support, including the use of office machines and computers.

Knowledgeable and adept at using computer office software programs to create and maintain reports, forms, and correspondence.

Assists individuals or groups with projects as assigned or on a regular basis. May have an area of special interest or knowledge that is assigned specifically.

Alternative Job Titles

Secretary, Office Manager, Project Assistant

Phrases for Duties

- Responsible for general office projects and assignments supporting one individual, a group, or a department.

- Answers phones and greets visitors and treats them in a professional manner. Directs calls to appropriate persons, or screens calls as directed. Uses judgment in interacting with the employees and customers.

- Answers correspondence, fills in forms, and generates other documents as needed using computer software programs.

- Operates a variety of office equipment, including phone systems, printers, faxes, and different types of computer applications.

- Schedules appointments, composes correspondence, manages calendars, and processes expense reports.
- May interact with vendors and purchase supplies and other department needs.
- Uses discretion in disseminating information. Is highly guarded with confidential information.
- Coordinates meetings and events with other personnel to ensure clear communications.
- Maintains records, databases, filing, and forms.

Customer Service Representative

Definition of Customer Service Representative

Interacts with customers to provide information in response to inquiries about products and services and to handle complaints.

Handles problems in a diplomatic manner, and attempts to satisfy the customers' needs.

Uses good judgment before directing calls to the next level.

Alternative Job Titles

Client Services Representative, Account Service Representative, Call Center Representative

Phrases for Duties

- Confers with customers by telephone or in person to provide information about products or services. Takes phone orders, cancels accounts, or deals with complaints or other issues.

- Keeps records of customer interactions and transactions, recording details of inquiries, complaints, and comments, as well as actions taken.

- Resolves customers' service or billing complaints by performing activities such as exchanging merchandise, refunding money, and adjusting bill.

- Checks to ensure that appropriate changes have been made to resolve customer problems.

➡

- Contacts customers to respond to inquiries or to notify them of claim investigation results and any planned adjustments.

- Directs unresolved customer grievances to designated departments for further investigation.

- Determines charges for services requested, collects deposits, payments, or arranges for billing.

- Completes contract forms, prepares change of address records, and issues service discontinuance orders by using computer.

- Obtains and examines all relevant information to assess validity of complaints and determines possible causes or other extenuating circumstances.

- Solicits sales of new or additional services or products.

Following are positions in **Office Management**. The descriptions included are for **Office Manager, Department Manager, Sales Manager**, **Project Manager, Product Manager**. Alternative titles are also listed.

Definition of Office Manager

Coordinates all office activities by directing support services.

Controls expenses and tracks productivity by supervising office clerical functions and jobs.

Delegates responsibility or performs clerical tasks as required.

Responsibilities can include the role of liaison with all outside vendors.

Alternative Job Titles

Administrative Manager, Administrative Coordinator, Department Manager

Phrases for Duties

- Directs or coordinates the supportive services of a business, agency, or organization, setting goals and implementing plans and schedules.

- Plans, administers, and controls budgets for contracts, equipment, and supplies according to level of responsibility and company policy.

- Oversees special projects to ensure that facilities meet environmental, health, and security standards and comply with government regulations.

- Works with other individuals to attract and hire qualified people who will add value to the department.

- Monitors performance of employees against standards and goals set.
- Follows procedures and works within company policy to improve performance of individual employees by providing improvement plans.
- Follows company policy to terminate employees for cause or for performance issues.
- Analyzes internal processes and recommends and implements procedural or policy changes to improve the efficiency of the operations.
- Outsources or oversees the maintenance and repair of machinery, equipment, and electrical and mechanical systems.
- Monitors the facility to ensure safety and security.

Department Manager

Definition of Department Manager

Directs and coordinates activities of workers in a
    department or branch.

Acts as information expert for a particular discipline
    such as accounting, human resources, maintenance,
    marketing, sales, or any other specific department
    within a company.

Alternative Job Titles

[Specific Department] Manager, e.g., Accounting Manager,
Branch Manager, Operations Manager

Phrases for Duties

- Identifies and communicates key responsibilities and
  practices to immediate team members to promote a
  successful attitude for teamwork.

- Develops programs and projects that support the
  department's role within the company.

- Coordinates and collaborates with internal and external
  sources to accomplish goals and meet deadlines.

- Manages expenses and budgets to ensure that
  programs are aligned with company business goals
  and objectives.

- Recruits, interviews, and hires staff members. Oversees
  training programs for employees.

➡

- Sets goals and standards for expected performance of employees. Plans, directs, and coordinates the activities of workers in branches, offices, or departments.

- Monitors employee performance against set goals and expectations.

- Networks within company, industry, or community to find and attract new business.

- Establishes and maintains relationships with individuals and business customers.

Sales Manager

Definition of Sales Manager

Directs the actual distribution or movement of a product or service to the customer.

Coordinates sales distribution by establishing sales territories, quotas, and goals, and establishes training programs for sales representatives.

Analyzes sales statistics gathered by staff members to determine sales potential and inventory requirements, and monitors the preferences of customers.

Alternative Job Titles

Director of Sales, District Sales Manager, Regional Sales Manager, Sales Supervisor, General Manager, Store Manager

Phrases for Duties

- Responsible for prospecting new accounts, qualifying and closing accounts, and maintaining existing customer relationships.

- Analyzes data analysis and confers with various department heads to plan advertising and marketing services to define the right target segments.

- Overseas all aspects of office groups and sales field staff. Plans and directs staffing, training, and performance evaluations to provide development and growth of staff.

- Monitors customer satisfaction and needs to determine focus of sales efforts. Resolves customer complaints regarding sales and service.

- Works with other sources within and outside the company to create, develop, and execute campaign materials.

- Analyzes campaign results and tunes them to generate best results, including ROI [return on investment], lead and call management, product mix, and reaching target audience.

- Prepares budgets, and approves or rejects budget expenditures. Determines price schedules and discount rates.

- May be hands-on and perform many functions to accomplish department goals and meet deadlines.

- May travel extensively or as needed.

Project Manager

Definition of Project Manager

Coordinates a project from inception to conclusion.

Involved throughout the project cycle, coordinating and managing the final execution of the project and project costs.

Responsible for tracking the project against the schedule. Also tracking the budget and phase review objectives.

Provides status reports to the customers and staff on a regular basis.

Alternative Job Titles

Project Manager I (II or III); [Specific Department] Project Manager, e.g., IT Project Manager, Marketing Project Manager; Senior Project Manager; Project Group Manager

Phrases for Duties

- Coordinates the work of individual team members throughout all phases of the project.

- Provides overall strategy and technical solutions as warranted for project challenges.

- Sets deadlines, assigns responsibilities, and monitors progress of project.

- Mentors and motivates the team, continuing to maintain good client relations throughout the project.

- Meets with other departments and resources on a regular basis. Travel may be involved.

- Provides written documentation and reports to all people and departments involved on the progress being made against the deadline.

- Tracks the financial aspects of the project, including the billing, account collection, and proposals.

- Presents before the client, executive committee, and any other outside entities.

Product Manager

Definition of Product Manager

Manages, develops, and implements product marketing activities.

Executes the vision of the brand and the product development process.

Partners with creative teams working collaboratively to plan and accomplish goals.

Leads and directs cross-functional activities.

Manages the work flow from conception to the final handoff of the product.

Develops product information and technical specifications.

Alternative Job Titles

Brand Manager; [Specific Department] Product Manager, e.g., Web Product Manager; Product Development Manager

Phrases for Duties

- Provides strategic recommendations to drive growth of products.
- Manages the product in all phases of development. Coordinates products throughout the life cycle, from strategic definition to end-of-life planning.
- Interfaces with the clients regarding deliverables. Makes recommendations on possible positioning and growth of the product.

- Works with and manages cross-functional teams.

- Is familiar with the standard concepts of product development, and positions the product, packaging, and pricing to be competitive with the market.

- Responsible for the approval of design development.

- Is aware of targeted market and the activities necessary to reach the market through packaging, pricing, and strategies to maximize sales.

- Works with other departments to develop product information and technical specifications.

- Plans steps and deadlines necessary to meet deadlines to take the product to market.

- Stays abreast of current trends and competition. Uses information to stay competitive in the cost and placement of goods.

- Seeks out new opportunities for product development.

Chapter 7

Positions in Various Industries and Fields

The following are descriptions of a number of positions in various industries and fields. Titles may vary from company to company, but the duties or responsibilities will fall into similar categories.

These are positions for **Design and Media** occupations. They include: **Graphic Designer, Technical Writer, Copywriter, Public Relations Specialist, Editor**. Alternative titles are also provided.

Graphic Designer

Definition of Graphic Designer

With originality and creativity, designs or creates graphics for Web sites, advertising, packaging, displays, logos, or whatever needs a customer has.

Uses a variety of mediums and technology.

Alternative Job Titles

Graphic Artist, Designer, Creative Manager, Desktop Publisher

Phrases for Duties

- Develops graphics and layouts for product illustrations, company logos, and Web sites.

- Works with customers to determine what needs they have and how to best work within their budgets. Confers with clients to discuss and determine layout design.

- Creates designs, concepts, and sample layouts based on knowledge of layout principles and esthetic design concepts. Customizes designs to fit the industry and culture of the company.

- Determines size and arrangement of illustrative material and copy. Selects styles and themes as well as fonts and sizes of type.

- Prepares illustrations or rough sketches of material, discussing them with clients or supervisors and making necessary changes.

- Uses advanced computer software to generate new images. Keeps up to date with the latest trends and technology options available.

- Works with other workers or vendors involved in the project, and provides instructions to make the final layouts for printing.

- Reviews final layouts and suggests improvements as needed.

- Maintains archive of resources: images, photos, or previous work products.

Technical Writer

Definition of Technical Writer

Writes a variety of technical documentation, including technical articles, reports, business proposals, and instructions.

Keeps current with trends and new technology to review and rewrite any existing documents for consistency and accuracy based on current information.

Uses many versions of software and hardware to reflect the latest developments in the field.

Works closely with other departments on the creation of materials and instructions.

Alternative Job Titles

Senior Technical Writer; Technical Writer I (II, III, or IV); Associate Technical Writer; Proposal Writer; [Specific Department] Technical Writer, e.g., IT Technical Writer, Military Technical Writer

Phrases for Duties

- Writes and edits documentation for a wide range of uses.
- Coordinates between departments and customers to organize projects and complete writing assignments.
- Creates and revises processes and documentation, including systems and associated databases.
- Creates, writes, and revises technical system training materials.

➡

- Reviews and revises existing documentation for consistency and accuracy based on current best practices.

- Confers with customers, vendors, and executives to ensure that specifications are correct and agreed upon.

- Selects photos and artwork or any other illustrations for printed materials.

- May interview other technical personnel for input and to work collaboratively on multimedia projects.

- Researches subject matter and products by reading journals and other materials to become familiar with the customers' businesses and the end products.

- Creates documents and methodology in detail, including step-by-step instructions.

- Researches applicable rules and standards as well as any audit points that may be required.

- Arranges for production of materials and troubleshoots any problems in order to expedite the process.

Copywriter

Definition of Copywriter

Researches, writes, and edits technical information by coordinating with other contributors to the publication.

Develops resources through research of current issues, trends, and economic and political climate.

Writes articles, bulletins, sales letters, speeches, and other related informative, marketing, and promotional material.

Writes in a style and manner that is consistent with the tone and quality of the organization's mission.

Acts as the coordinator of information to collect facts and data and to produce creative products to satisfy customers' needs to be "best in class."

Alternative Job Titles

Business Writer, Web Content Writer, Copywriter/Editor, Creative Writer, Copyeditor

Phrases for Duties

- Uses outside resources and develops creative writing to sell a variety of products and services.
- Writes advertising copy for use in publications, broadcasts, or Internet media, to promote the sale of goods and services.
- Uses direct marketing, online advertising, and Web exposure to drive results.

➡

- Works directly with clients to identify business needs and ideas.

- Consults with sales, media, and marketing representatives to obtain information on product or service and to discuss methods of dissemination, style, and length of written copy.

- Edits or rewrites existing copy as necessary, and submits copy for approval by customers and any other team members or management who are involved in the project.

- Act as liaison between the company and the customers to ensure that all expectations are on track, checking periodically for feedback.

- Communicates to customers in their terms, and on their level, so that the advertiser's sales message is received.

- Creates names and images and writes advertising copy for packaging, brochures, and other promotional materials.

- Stays abreast of the latest trends in media and advertising to promote products in a competitive manner.

Public Relations Specialist

Definition of Public Relations Specialist

Prepares and disseminates information regarding an organization through newspapers, journals, television, radio, the Internet, and all other forms of media to promote sales and services.

Writes proposals, and prepares contracts.

May also negotiate contracts with potential customers.

Performs a variety of tasks and works with a broad range of media: Web development, brochures, broadcasting, publications.

Uses creative license according to the specifications of the job.

Engages in promoting or creating goodwill for individuals, groups, or organizations by writing or selecting favorable publicity material and releasing it through various communications media.

Alternative Job Titles

Public Affairs Specialist, Community Relations Specialist, Information and Communications Specialist, Media Coordinator

Phrases for Duties

- Prepares or edits organizational publications for internal and external audiences, including employee newsletters and stockholders' reports.

- Prepares and disseminates information through newspapers, journals, television, radio, the Internet, and all other forms of media to promote sales and services.

- Responds to requests for information from the media, or designates another appropriate spokesperson.

- Establishes and maintains relationships with representatives of the community, employees, the press, and any public interest groups.

- Plans and directs development and communication of public interest or informational programs to maintain favorable community outreach.

- Arranges public appearances, lectures, contests, or exhibits for clients to increase product and service awareness and to promote goodwill.

- Studies the objectives, promotional policies, and needs of organizations to develop public relations strategies that will influence public opinion or promote ideas, products, and services.

- Coaches client representatives about effective communication with the public and with employees.

- Plans and organizes publicity events within set budget guidelines.

Definition of Editor

Oversees the design and content of publications or Web sites.

Performs variety of editorial duties, such as laying out, indexing, and revising content of written materials.

Reviews all assignments before publication to ensure that all documents are accurate and meet established content standards.

May direct and lead the work of others: writers, freelancers, and research assistants.

Alternative Job Titles

Managing Editor, Senior Editor, Communications Editor, Project Editor, News Editor, Sports Editor, Feature Editor, Web Content Editor

Phrases for Duties

- Responsible for one or more specific programs, including content, schedules, budget, and project planning.

- Works with subject matter experts to extract information to write and edit content.

- Acts as liaison to manage internal and external writers and experts. Assigns topics, events, and stories to individual writers for coverage.

- Works with management and editorial staff to plan content and placement with emphasis on developing stories.

- Uses exceptional attention to detail and ability to multitask to track progress of projects and keep other members informed.

- Oversees publication production, including artwork, layout, and printing, to ensure adherence to deadlines.

- Confers with management and editorial staff members regarding placement and emphasis of developing news stories.

Position descriptions in this section are for **Human Resources (HR)** and include: **Human Resources Assistant, Employment Coordinator, Compensation and Benefits Specialist, Human Resources Manager, Training and Development Specialist**. Alternative titles are also listed.

Human Resources Assistant

Definition of Human Resources Assistant

Provides support in all areas of the human resources department, which may include recruitment, compensation, benefits, training, compliance, selection, orientation, and employee relations.

Responsible for maintaining all personnel records, entering personnel information into a database.

Has access to highly confidential files and information. Provides information to authorized persons following company policy and procedures.

Alternative Job Titles

Human Resources Coordinator, Human Resources Associate, Human Resources Representative

Phrases for Duties

- Supports administration, coordination, and application of companywide human resources policies and procedures.
- Organizes and maintains confidential files and records.
- Assists in day-to-day recruiting, including reviewing applications, scheduling interviews, and maintaining all job board postings.
- Performs general clerical duties, including filing, photocopying, faxing, and mailing.

- Assists with communication of group insurance and other benefit programs, and processes any changes or updates to employees' files. Processes and coordinates paperwork related to benefits.
- Effectively handles multiple assignments and special projects and other duties as assigned.

Employment Coordinator

Definition of Employment Coordinator

Plans and implements recruiting efforts to maintain staffing needs.

Interviews job applicants, and refers qualified candidates to prospective employers for consideration.

Tracks employment requisitions and conducts background and reference checks.

Coordinates offer letters and pre-employment drug screenings.

Ensures compliance with state and federal regulations and human resources policies and procedures.

May also be responsible for new employee orientation.

Alternative Job Titles

Staffing Coordinator, Employment Representative, Employment Service Specialist, Personnel Coordinator, Recruiter

Phrases for Duties

■ Develops strategic recruitment and employment programs to attract the best qualified candidates to present to hiring managers.

■ Recruits and interviews applicants, assessing qualifications and fit with the position, department, and organization.

■ Provides excellent customer service to internal and external customers. Building relationships to understand the staffing needs.

- Monitors response of candidates to job postings and ads, adjusting as needed.

- Processes applications of qualified candidates in a nondiscriminatory manner.

- Coordinates interviews and follow-up with candidate and interviewers and hiring manager.

- Informs applicants of the details and responsibilities of the position, compensation, benefits, schedules, working conditions, and promotion opportunities.

- Performs reference and background checks, including drug testing, as mandated by company policy.

- Maintains records of applicants not selected for employment.

- May perform general clerical duties as required.

Compensation and Benefits Specialist

Definition of Compensation and Benefits Specialist

Conducts and participates in compensation surveys.

Assists in plan design and changes.

Monitors, maintains, and analyzes company benefits program for competitiveness against budget restrictions.

Participates in annual merit review cycle for all eligible employees.

Assists with periodic audits.

Alternative Job Titles

Compensation Analyst, Human Resources Analyst, Benefits Analyst, Benefits Specialist, Benefits Administrator, Benefits Manager, Compensation/Benefits Specialist

Phrases for Duties

- Assists in the development of the employee benefits plans and the organization's compensation program.
- Conducts market and equity analysis, analyzes data, and prepares recommendations.
- Responds to all inquiries regarding medical, dental, life, optional life, short-term and long-term disability, vision plans, and flexible spending accounts (FSAs).
- Serves as liaison with third-party administrator and employees to resolve any problems with claims or eligibility.

➡

- Handles funding of medical claims and flexible spending accounts.

- Assists in the renewal and negotiation process for annual enrollment.

- Assists with periodic audits and compliance with any state or federal agencies.

- Prepares recommendations to address equity and any compensation-related factors.

- Maintain a supply of all benefit forms, booklets, and informational materials, and make them available and accessible to employees.

Human Resources Manager

Definition of Human Resources Manager

Supports the execution of human resources initiatives to include staffing, training, performance management, employee relations, and HR communications, including policies and procedures.

Responsible for the development of the HR department goals, objectives, policies, and systems.

Alternative Job Titles

Human Resources Director, Generalist

Phrases for Duties

- Develops the HR department goals, objectives, and systems.
- Develops and monitors an annual budget that includes HR services, employee recognition, and administration.
- Responsible for preparing key HR-related statistical reports and other periodic reports for management.
- Participates in department head meetings and staff meetings and attends other meetings and seminars, monitoring HR-related issues.
- Leads compliance with all existing government and labor legal reporting requirements, and is responsible for the preparation of information requested or required for compliance with laws.

- Responsible for performance management and improvement systems combined with employee services and counseling.

- Reviews recommendations for employment terminations, and guides department heads about them. Participates in investigations. Abides by zero tolerance for abuse and noncompliance with state and federal mandated laws.

- Conducts employee complaint investigations when brought forth. Reviews employee appeals through the complaint procedures.

- Establishes and leads the standard recruiting and hiring practices and procedures necessary to recruit and hire a superior workforce.

- Establishes wage and salary structure, and leads competitive market research to pay practices and pay bands that help recruit and retain superior staff.

- Defines all HR training programs. Provides department heads, managers, and employees with necessary education and materials, including workshops, manuals, employee handbooks, and standardized reports.

Training and Development Specialist

Definition of Training and Development Specialist

Designs and conducts company training programs.

Coordinates training materials used for educating employees.

Supervises a team of trainers, making sure that the integrity and the quality of the training programs are up to expectations for the group.

Alternative Job Titles

Corporate Trainer, Job Training Specialist, Management Development Specialist, Trainer, Training Coordinator, Training Specialist

Phrases for Duties

- Responsible for the facilitation and delivery of coursework and programs for management and employees.
- Collaborates with supervisors to ensure successful implementation of a variety of training programs.
- May supervise a team of trainers who are responsible for developing the training materials for classroom, on-the-job, or individual training programs.
- Ensures coordination of highly specialized training to smaller segments of the user groups supported, including new hire classes.

➥

- Collaborates with supervisors to ensure successful implementation of a variety of training programs.

- Supports the execution of training test plans and the development of corresponding training materials.

- Sets expectations for managing the performance of trainers.

- Stays up to date on business issues and new product and service developments pertinent to training.

The following are positions in the area of **Finance and Accounting**. Titles included are: **Accountant, Budget Analyst, Auditor, Financial Analyst, Loan Officer**. Alternative titles are also included.

Accountant

Definition of Accountant

Reviews financial information and account activities.

Responsible for the overall account analysis and reconciliation as well as the preparation of financial statements.

Prepares financial reports on assets, liabilities, profit and loss, tax liability, and other financial activities.

Assists with the annual budget process and financial audit.

Alternative Job Titles

Staff Accountant I (II, III, or IV), Cost Accountant, Senior Accountant, Property Tax Accountant, Fixed Asset Accountant, Certified Public Accountant (CPA)

Phrases for Duties

- Prepares quarterly and annual financial statements. Analyzes accounting records, financial statements, and other financial reports for internal and external users.

- Collects data and is responsible for the accuracy, completeness, and consistency of reporting financial records.

- Prepares balance sheets, profit and loss statements, and other financial reports.

- Responsible for analyzing trends, costs, revenues, financial commitments, and obligations incurred to predict future revenues and expenses.

- Reports organization's finances to management, and offers suggestions about resource utilization, tax strategies, and underlying budget forecasts.

- Determines and implements cost accounting procedures and methods, and examines and reviews unusual cost records to make sure that cost data is allocated correctly.

- Ensures that all reporting is in compliance with the Securities and Exchange Commission (SEC) and other reporting guidelines by researching and following accounting rules and regulations.

- Makes recommendations regarding company policies and compliance issues.

- Assists external auditors, as needed.

- Computes taxes owed and prepares tax returns, ensuring compliance with tax requirements.

Budget Analyst

Definition of Budget Analyst

Actively assists in financial management by performing budget analysis.

Prepares portions of annual budget and operating plans, designs, and computer databases.

Prepares various financial reports and compiles data for fiscal year submissions.

Alternative Job Titles

Financial Analyst/Budget Analyst, Budget Analyst I (II, III, or IV), Senior Budget Analyst, Federal Budget Analyst

Phrases for Duties

- Analyzes accounting records to determine financial resources required to implement programs.
- Makes recommendations for budget allocations to ensure that budgetary limits are being followed.
- Periodically reviews operating budgets and analyzes trends and changes that affect budget needs and controls.
- Evaluates accounting data to resolve transactions, monitor balances, and ensure the proper management of funds.
- Maintains accurate and timely financial information in financial system and database to facilitate reporting requirements.

- Directs the preparation of regular and special budget reports.

- Supports paperwork for annual audit, monthly invoices, and quarterly reports.

- Provides analysis and documentation demonstrating program performance.

Auditor

Definition of Auditor

Analyzes accounting and financial data of various departments to determine status of accounts.

Ensures accuracy and seeks out any discrepancies in accounting procedures.

Responsible for making recommendations to ensure compliance with government guidelines and laws.

Works with outside auditors to help reconcile discrepancies or support the external auditing function.

Alternative Job Titles

Internal Auditor, Lead Auditor, Audit Manager, Financial Auditor, Auditor I (II, III, or IV)

Phrases for Duties

- Conducts assigned audits of company operations and practices to ensure compliance with policies, plans, procedures, laws, and regulations.
- Provides guidance to management regarding asset utilization and audit results.
- Analyzes data to detect deficient controls or extravagant, fraudulent, and noncompliance activity or behavior.
- Documents the results of all phases of the audit preparing financial reports and paperwork to ensure that findings and recommendations are properly supported.

- Assists with assessing risk, makes recommendations to improve operations or strengthen business controls, and negotiates solutions.

- Conducts interviews with auditors to resolve questions.

- Represents the department as a business partner to assist all company activities.

- Encourages management to use audit services for assistance.

- Assists in planning and executing special audit projects as assigned.

Financial Analyst

Definition of Financial Analyst

Supports managers in financial control by providing financial analyses for business planning and decision making.

Compiles and analyzes financial information. Develops integrated revenue and expense analyses, projections, reports, and presentations.

Alternative Job Titles

Financial Analyst I (II, III, or IV), Business Systems Analyst, Securities Analyst, Planning Analyst, Research Analyst

Phrases for Duties

- Creates and analyzes monthly, quarterly, and annual reports and ensures that financial information has been recorded accurately.

- Conducts quantitative analyses of information affecting investment programs of public or private institutions.

- Prepares, analyzes, and reports actual results against project operating plans, including sales, margins, receivables, inventory, capital, and headcount.

- Performs monthly close process activities, including the preparation of required accounting entries, accruals, and account reconciliations.

- Leads the analysis of monthly results of sales, revenue, and expenses. Prepares monthly rolling forecasts and cost/profit analyses.

➡

- Supports proposal preparation, and assists in preparation of financial budgets and operating plans.

- Identifies trends and developments in competitive environments, and presents findings to management.

- Disseminates and explains sales and revenue results to user groups and management.

- Maintains knowledge and stays abreast of developments in the fields of industrial technology, business, finance, and economic theory.

- Performs financial forecasting and reconciliation of internal accounts.

- Supports auditor and accounting requests for financial reports and analyses.

Loan Officer

Definition of Loan Officer

Originates and evaluates residential mortgage loans and credit loans.

Recommends approval or denial of loans.

Advises borrowers of rights, obligations, and payment responsibilities.

Develops leads from assigned sources.

Participates in various business development activities to contact potential clients.

Works to retain existing business.

Alternative Job Titles

Mortgage Loan Officer, Commercial Loan Officer, Financial Specialist, Branch Lending Officer

Phrases for Duties

- Develops and services consumer loans, including auto, residential mortgage, and unsecured personal loans.

- Cultivates relationships with previous and new customers via company-provided leads as well as self-generated telemarketing campaigns.

- Analyzes and determines clients' needs, and conveys what resources are available to them as loan applicants.

- Responsible for all aspects of the loan process, including the coordination of documents: client application, appraisal information, and title reports.

- Analyzes applicants' financial status, credit, and property evaluations to determine feasibility of granting loans.

- Explains to customers the different types of loans and credit options that are available, as well as the terms of those services.

- Works within lender submission guidelines and loan funding regulations.

- Provides excellent customer service while fulfilling mortgage needs of the applicant.

- Reviews and updates credit and loan files.

- Negotiates terms of loan financing based on client qualifications.

- Stays abreast of new types of loans and other financial services and products to better meet customers' needs.

The positions in the next category are **Computer Industry** jobs. They include: **Computer Programmer, Data Security Specialist, Computer Systems Analyst, Database Administrator, Network Systems and Data Communications Analyst.** Alternative titles are included.

Computer Programmer

Definition of Computer Programmer

Familiar with a variety of the field's concepts, practices, and procedures.

Reviews, analyzes, and modifies programming systems, including encoding, testing, debugging, and documenting programs.

Develops and writes computer programs using commonly used concepts, practices, and procedures within a particular field.

Converts project specifications and statements of problems and procedures into computer language. May program Web sites.

Alternative Job Titles

Programmer; Program Analyst; Software Developer; Specific Programmer, e.g., Linux Systems Programmer, C Programmer, SQL Programmer, Web Software Programmer

Phrases for Duties

- Writes, analyzes, reviews, and makes changes to programs using various methods, while applying subject matter and symbolic logic.

- Converts documented client needs into program code following established standards and practices.

- Conducts testing of programs and appropriate software to meet needs while providing "user-friendly" instructions.

➡

- Documents applications and systems in order to define the technical process.
- Delivers written descriptions, flowcharts, or segments.
- Writes or contributes to writing instructions or manuals to guide end users.
- Uses coding to produce understandable instructions.
- Corrects any errors to existing programs to complete desired programs.
- Consults with engineering and technical personnel to clarify program intent, identify problems, and suggest changes.
- Performs revisions, repairs, or expansions of existing programs to increase operating efficiency or adapt to new requirements.

Data Security Specialist

Definition of Data Security Analyst

Maintains systems to protect data from unauthorized users. Plans, coordinates, and implements security measures for information systems to regulate access.

Identifies and resolves or reports security violations.

Alternative Job Titles

Data Security Analyst, Computer Security Systems Specialist, Security Specialist

Phrases for Duties

- Consults on the development of business systems and troubleshooting support.
- Acts as liaison between departments translating business requirements into effective systems designs.
- Develops plans to safeguard computer files against accidental or unauthorized modification, destruction, or disclosure and to meet emergency data processing needs.
- Assists in the evaluation, development, and effectiveness of systems, policies, and emergency responses.
- Participates in the development of management information in business organizations.
- Monitors current reports of computer viruses to determine when to update virus protection systems.

- Modifies computer security files to incorporate new software, correct errors, or change individual access status.

- Performs risk assessments and executes tests of data processing system to ensure functioning of data processing activities and security measures.

Computer Systems Analyst

Definition of Computer Systems Analyst

Reviews and analyzes information security systems and users' needs.

Recommends applications and develops procedures to improve existing systems.

Documents requirements, defines scope and objectives, and formulates systems.

Works closely with internal and external project teams to ensure that projects are delivered on schedule.

May analyze or recommend commercially available software.

May supervise computer programmers.

Alternative Job Titles

Data Systems Analyst, Desk Top Systems Analyst, Senior Programmer Analyst

Phrases for Duties

- Designs, develops, tests, and deploys integrations.
- Manages data mapping systems and works with detection of system weaknesses and corrections.
- Responsible for standard integrations with other external IT systems, policies, and servers.
- Responsible for computer security and keeping computers operating at peak performance through proactive maintenance programs.

- Consults with management and technical staff to ensure agreement on system principles to expand or modify system.

- Responsible for assisting staff and users with computer and program-related problems.

Database Administrator

Definition of Database Administrator

Responsible for the development, administration, and maintenance of database policies and procedures.

Guarantees the security and integrity of the company database by planning and coordinating security measures.

Implements database policies.

Resolves issues with database performance, capacity issues, or any other data issues.

Alternative Job Titles

Database Analyst, Database Coordinator, Database Programmer, Information Systems Manager

Phrases for Duties

- Researches, recommends, implements, and manages appropriate changes and system updates and upgrades.
- Installs, configures, and maintains database software.
- Provides documentation support relating to the maintenance of systems to ensure company compliance with regulations.
- Tests programs or databases, corrects errors, and makes necessary modifications.
- Provides excellent customer service and delivery of technological services.

- Provides key database and application redundancy of technological services.
- Manages and prioritizes multiple projects simultaneously to meet management mandated deadlines.
- Develops guidelines for the use and acquisition of software.

Network Systems and Data Communications Analyst

Definition of Network Systems and Data Communications Analyst

Reviews, analyzes, and evaluates network systems, such as local area networks.

Performs network modeling, analysis, and planning.

Documents requirements, defines scope and objectives, and formulates systems to parallel overall business strategies.

Alternative Job Titles

Network Systems Analyst I (II or III), Business Systems Analyst I (II or III), Applications Systems Analyst I (II or III), Network Administrator

Phrases for Duties

- Maintains and modifies application software and packages via vendors' engineering releases and utilities.

- Evaluates and documents current manual and/or automated systems in preparation for system conversion, initial implementation, or maintenance.

- Establishes acceptable action plans for application software projects, recommends team members, and assigns responsibilities.

- Designs and documents general functional requirements and detailed technical specifications for application software consistent with regional standards and departmental policies.

➡

- Ensures data integrity through interaction with financial and outcomes systems and auditing verification.

- Complies with and supports enforcement of confidentiality of protected health information policies at all times.

- Tests new and/or modified applications software in accordance with established acceptance criteria.

- Installs and implements application software in an optimal manner to minimize the effect on production and development activities.

- Complies with departmental change management processes at all times.

- Provides effective direction to project team members, or other staff members, and assists in coordinating activities, including project management.

- Analyzes clients' needs regarding new or enhanced systems applications and software.

- Interacts with users and clients through various phases of analysis, design, implementation, and maintenance.

- Ensures that clients are trained on new enhancements.

- Demonstrates the organization's core values of respect, justice, compassion, and excellence to customers, employees, and visitors; provides quality service in the performance of work assignments and duties.

- Maintains established departmental policies, procedures, and objectives, improving organization performance program and safety standards.

- Communicates project status and operational changes with managers and staff, as appropriate.

➡

- Maintains professional growth and development through seminars, workshops, and professional affiliations to keep abreast of latest trends in field of expertise.
- Attends meetings as required, and participates on committees as directed. Represents the IT department in a professional manner at all times.
- Performs other duties as assigned.

Following are job titles in the **Health Care Industry** and include: **Dental Hygienist/Dental Assistant, Medical Assistant, Physical Therapist, Dietetic Technician, Radiologic Technician**. Alternative titles are included.

Dental Hygienist/Dental Assistant

Definition of Dental Hygienist

Uses dental instruments to clean and remove stains from patients' teeth.

Checks patients' oral health by examining for various problems, including oral cancer.

May provide clinical services and health education to improve and maintain health for schoolchildren.

May conduct clinical group dental health sessions to community groups.

Definition of Dental Assistant

Assists dentist in a variety of procedures, including oral surgery.

Prepares and sterilizes instruments, hands to dentist the necessary tools, and provides assistance during patient treatment.

May record findings.

Alternative Job Titles

Orthodontic Assistant, Surgical Dental Assistant, Registered Dental Hygienist

Phrases for Duties

- Prepares treatment room for patient, ensuring that prescribed procedures and protocols are followed.

- Prepares patients for treatment by welcoming, soothing, seating, and draping them.
- Provides information to patients by answering questions and requests.
- Maintains instruments and equipment by sterilizing, disinfecting, and sharpening instruments.
- Follows standard precautions using personal protective equipment, as required.
- Performs x-rays and develops films.
- Completes dental procedures of cleaning and examining patients' teeth and gums.
- Checks for indications of disease or possible problems.
- Records treatment information in patient records.
- Instructs patients in oral hygiene and plaque control programs.
- Conducts dental education clinics for schools and general public health events, educating children and adults on the care of teeth and good oral hygiene.
- Performs all procedures in compliance with the dental practice act.

Medical Assistant

Definition of Medical Assistant

Assists in the examination and treatment of patients. Interviews patients, measures vital signs, and records information on patients' charts.

May administer injections and draw and collect blood samples from patients to be forwarded to a laboratory for analysis.

Performs administrative assignments, such as scheduling appointments and making phone calls, to remind patients of appointments.

May also maintain medical records, billing, and coding for insurance purposes.

Alternative Job Titles

Physician Assistant–Medical, Medical Office Assistant, Clinical Assistant

Phrases for Duties

- Directs patients to proper exam/treatment room; accurately obtains and documents vitals.

- Prepares patients for examinations and other procedures. Assists physician with procedures as directed.

- Instructs patients in all appropriate procedures and directions for home use.

- Maintains, cleans, and/or sterilizes medical and laser equipment.
- Prepares and administers medications for injections.
- Handles the disposal of infectious and/or hazardous waste; cleans.
- Collects, labels, and documents specimens, and transports them to the laboratory.
- Screens pharmaceutical representatives. Maintains sample closet; disposes of expired samples, and reports needed supplies to appropriate personnel.
- Posts and updates schedules; obtains necessary charts, and enters proper billing codes into practice management system.
- Performs referral duties as needed.

Definition of Physical Therapist

Evaluates and assesses needs of referred patients.

Formulates and implements the training plan for treatment.

Provides therapy services defined in treatment plan.

Works with physicians, case managers, and adjustors to treat rehabilitative cases.

Monitors progress of improved strength and relief of pain.

Alternative Job Titles

Nursing Home Physical Therapist, Home Care Physical Therapist, Outpatient Physical Therapist, Registered Physical Therapist

Phrases for Duties

- Provides therapy services defined in treatment plans.
- Works cooperatively with physician to document evaluations and diagnoses.
- Prepares plans and modifies care to meet goals of physical therapy interventions.
- Physically administers any treatment necessary to aid in the recovery or pain relief process.
- Keeps documentation of initial exams and treatment schedules.

- Tracks progress and improvements as to strength and lack of pain.
- Communicates with physician or others involved regarding progress and need for further treatments or reevaluation.

Dietetic Technician

Definition of Dietetic Technician

Using scoring guidelines, identifies patients with nutritional risk.

Under the supervision of dietitians, initiates referrals for dietetic assessment.

Plans basic nutritional needs, including individualized menus, by calculating calorie count results.

Teaches principles of food and nutrition, or counsels individuals.

Alternative Job Titles

Diet Technician, Nutrition Technician

Phrases for Duties

- Assists dietitians in the provision of food service and nutritional programs for patients with special diets.

- Interviews patients and formulates nutritional status and history.

- Establishes patients' charts after initial screening.

- Gives patients instructions on restricted diets, such as sodium restricted diets or diets for controlling cholesterol, and food and drug interactions.

- Initiates dietary assessments.

- Monitors patients' conditions and progress, and reevaluates treatments as necessary.

- Enters progress notes on charts as treatment progresses.

- Plans and writes special menus based on established guidelines.

- Solves problems dealing with procedures, or answers questions when patients call in for advice.

- May conduct normal nutrition and general health-care classes for patients.

Radiologic Technician

Definition of Radiologic Technician

Provides radiologic work task coverage.

Performs radiation and contamination surveys for facilities and work tasks.

Conducts evaluations to determine employees' exposure to radiation.

Maintains compliance with applicable local, state, national, and laboratory regulations, procedures, and practices relative to radiologic control.

Alternative Job Titles

X-Ray Technician, Radiologic Control Technician, Nuclear Pharmacy Technician

Phrases for Duties

- Applies basic to midlevel radiologic protection in a nuclear environment working with more experienced coworkers carrying out assigned support for operation.

- Performs radiologic survey of work areas and personnel using the calibration of radiologic equipment.

- Works in a radiologic and hazardous work environment, which requires the wearing of specific respirators and full-body protection.

- Evaluates and removes radiologic-contaminated soil.

- Works directly with customers to communicate radiation safety information, clarifying radiation protection program authorization requirements, and facilitating problem solving.

- Performs varied and difficult tasks in reducing potential radiation hazards and supporting compliance with radiation protection program authorizations.

- Assists in the design and development of equipment used to measure or control radiation hazards; assists in the design of safety features; recommends appropriate monitors, working times, etc.; collects data; and drafts reports.

- In the field, performs varied and difficult tasks in reducing potential radiation hazards and supporting compliance with radiation protection program authorization.

- Processes film and evaluates it for technical quality and accurate patient identification and side labeling.

The following are positions in the **Community and Social Services** field. Titles in this section include: **Public Health – Case Social Worker, Vocational and School Counselor, Rehabilitation Counselor, Home Health Aide**. Alternative titles are included.

Public Health-Care Social Worker

Definition Public Health-Care Social Worker

Interviews and coordinates plans and programs to meet the social and emotional needs of patients and their families.

Provides support and crisis intervention, and assists families to cope with chronic, acute, or terminal illnesses.

Helps the family to understand the implications and complexities of the situation and the impact on their lives.

Provides patient counseling and referrals for other social services.

Alternative Job Titles

Medical Social Worker, Mental Health Professional, Clinical Social Worker, Case Worker–Home Care, Behavioral Health Specialist

Phrases for Duties

- Provides families with treatment, including therapy, skills training, and education, to enable them to care for their mentally ill or emotionally disturbed family members in the home.

- Works closely with other mental health specialists, such as psychiatrists, psychologists, clinical social workers, case managers, psychiatric nurses, school counselors, and behavioral health providers.

- Provides individual, family, and/or group counseling services to children, adolescents, and families.
- Documents work of diagnostic evaluations, progress notes, treatment plans, discharge procedures, and other consumer-related activities.
- Actively participates in clinical team and staff meetings.
- Communicates effectively and works cooperatively with employees, families, schools, individuals, and the public.
- Provides clinical counseling in community settings, when applicable.
- Shares in the 24-hour crisis assessments.
- Collaborates with other professionals to evaluate patients' medical or physical condition and to assess clients' needs.
- Adheres to and upholds the ethical standards of the profession.

Vocational and School Counselor

Definition of Vocational and School Counselor

Counsels individuals and gives guidance or advice.

Conducts one-on-one or group educational or vocational classes.

Provides resource services to students.

Interacts with parents of students, as warranted.

Alternative Job Titles

Counselor, Guidance Counselor, School Counselor, Career Counselor, Academic Counselor, Career Center Director

Phrases for Duties

- Serves as primary source of information for students, counselors, faculty, and administrators.

- Advises students regarding choices for college entry, career planning, and class selection.

- Counsels students with issues or problems regarding grades, attendance, social interaction, financial burdens, employment, or any policy infractions.

- Works with new or transferring students to provide information and resources to assure a smooth transition into the program.

- Leads workshops and seminars to develop community outreach programs to assist in the recruiting efforts to attract new students.

- Maintains accurate and complete student records according to district policies, school practices, and any laws or regulations.

- Coordinates any communication necessary between parents or guardians and other counselors and teachers regarding student behavior problems.

- Maintains vigilance regarding any possible abuse of children either while in school or outside of school. Uses good judgment in seeking out professional or legal assistance to report any problems observed.

- Encourages students or parents to seek additional assistance from mental health professionals when necessary.

Rehabilitation Counselor

Definition of Rehabilitation Counselor

Provides vocational rehabilitation services to disabled individuals.

Evaluates patients' qualifications and limitations to develop employment objectives.

Counsels individuals to determine interests and mental attitudes toward vocational change.

Assesses clients' lifestyles and personal situations, and implements rehabilitation programs and training.

Coordinates activities with other vocational professionals as well as caregivers and treatment facility staff members.

Alternative Job Titles

Vocational Rehabilitation Counselor, Rehabilitation Specialist, Vocational Counselor, Work Development Counselor, Psychiatric Rehabilitation Counselor

Phrases for Duties

- Conducts individual and group counseling and teaching programs.
- Provides information for participants on vocational resources and Web sites for information on new jobs.
- Monitors and records clients' progress to ensure that goals and objectives are met.

- Assesses client's readiness and determination to set goals and use resources to plan a new vocational path.
- Arranges for evaluations of clients' physical, mental, and vocational abilities.
- Confers with clients to discuss their options and goals so that rehabilitation programs and plans for accessing needed services can be developed.
- Analyzes information and develops a rehabilitation plan tailored to the clients' abilities, education, physical capabilities, and skill levels.
- Provides case management to ensure that services are being utilized, including program services and treatment within the agency or with other professionals.
- Prepares and maintains records and case files, including documentation such as clients' personal and eligibility information, services provided, narratives of client contacts, and relevant correspondence.
- Provides ongoing support and counseling as necessary.

Home Health Aide

Definition of Home Health Aide

Provides a high level of nursing assistant care for patients.

Coordinates the overall interdisciplinary plan of care for patients, from admission to discharge in a home care environment.

Alternative Job Titles

Home Care Staff Nurse, Home Health Provider, Case Worker–Home Care, Case Manager–Home Care

Phrases for Duties

- Acts as the liaison between patient, family, and home care personnel to ensure that necessary care is provided promptly and efficiently.

- May provide assistance and companionship by walking exercise, preparing meals, and taking a general interest in the patient.

- Maintains records of patients' care, condition, progress, or problems to report and discuss observations with supervisor or case manager.

- Provides patients and families with emotional support and instruction in areas such as caring for infants, preparing healthy meals, living independently, or adapting to disability or illness.

- Plans, purchases, and prepares to serve meals to patients or other family members, according to prescribed diets.

- Directs patients in simple prescribed exercises or in the use of braces or artificial limbs.
- Checks patients' pulse, temperature, and respiration. Changes dressings.
- Performs a variety of duties as requested by clients, such as obtaining household supplies or running errands.

Part Four

How to Write a Successful Job Posting or Ad

This part deals with the marketing of your posting or ad to reach the desired candidate to fill your position.

As with any item you wish to sell, you must appeal to the correct audience or market. The method, technique, or media that you use will depend on past practices by your company; budget allotted for the project; and time urgency.

Unlike the somewhat limited methods used before the popularity of the Internet, technology today offers a variety of outreach media allowing you a broader reach to other cities, states, and countries, simultaneously.

Along with the benefits of the rich resources available to you, come the bad things that will pose challenges in using the right media to find the right experienced person for your job. Only through trial and error will you be able to determine which media works best for your situation.

Chapter 8

Reaching the Right Candidate

The local newspaper is no longer the number one recruiting tool it once was. Although the Classifieds or Help Wanted sections of newspapers still exist, the arrival of the Internet has changed the way employers now reach out to candidates.

The use of the Internet across the nation and beyond has become the most efficient and popular way to recruit potential candidates to apply for your job opening.

There are many reasons to use online postings to attract a large number of applicants. If your job is a very specialized position that requires unique skills or a difficult-to-locate candidate, there are other methods of reaching specific groups such as industry journals that can be used to reach out to these special populations.

The rules for writing a job posting or ad are somewhat similar to those for writing the job description.

Writing the Job Posting or Ad

The job description will be the best recruiting tool that you can use to write a job posting. If you have followed the steps to write a perfect job description, you can now take that information and transfer it to your job posting.

Here are some basic guidelines to get you through the process of writing an informative and enticing job posting.

Specific Title of the Position

The job applicant will use the title of the position to find your posting when he or she is doing a career search. Because titles vary from company to company, it is best to be specific about your position's title or you may post it under more than one title.

A benefit of using the Internet is the ability to post under more than one title. Posting multiple times is an effective way to track responses for the same position. You can vary the title and the contact information and track the responses to determine which key words are attracting more job seekers than others. We'll continue to use our Human Resources Manager position that we discussed in Chapter 5, but we'll make some specific changes to the posting

Example

Human Resources Manager—Other titles used to post: Human Resources Director (HR Director), Employee Benefits Manager, Employee Relations Manager

Company Information

For many reasons, one of them being fraudulent advertising, some job seekers are very suspicious about giving out personal information on job postings. For this reason, your position should include company information that links to your company's Web site.

This is also an opportunity to include information about your company's mission, size, values, or what type of culture or environment that you offer.

Example

The XYZ Company is seeking an HR Manager to join our Human Resources Department. At XYZ Company, talented, dedicated employees are the most important element in achieving and maintaining our excellent standards as a premier health-care facility. We provide an enjoyable and satisfying work environment, as evidenced by the significant number of persons with 20 or more years of employment.

Job Description: Duties

The job duties identified in your job description will assist you in defining and writing this portion of the posting.

Example

Human Resources Manager

Short Overview Version

As a result of continuing growth, a Human Resources position is available that offers excellent advancement potential for an outgoing and enthusiastic career-minded individual with an entrepreneurial flare. This is a hands-on role that supports a busy operation.

This is an HR Generalist position responsible for managing the Human Resources functions: Employee Relations, Training, Recruitment, Worker's Compensation and Disability Management, Compensation and Benefits, and ensuring compliance with HR policies and procedures as well as federal, state, and local regulations.

Longer, Detailed Version

Human Resources Manager Responsibilities

- Development of the Human Resources department: goals, objectives, and systems.
- Develops and monitors an annual budget that includes Human Resources services, employee recognition, and administration. Responsible for preparing key HR-related statistical reports and other periodic reports for management, as necessary or requested, to track strategic goal accomplishment.
- Participates in department head and staff meetings, and attends other meetings and seminars, monitoring HR-related issues.

Policies and Procedures

- Coordinates and implements services, policies, and programs through Human Resources staff; reports to the Administrator and serves on the department head team;

assists and advises department heads about Human Resources issues.

- Partners with Administrator and CFO to communicate Human Resources policies, procedures, programs, and laws, and recommends changes to policies and objectives with regard to employee relations.

- Leads compliance with all existing governmental and labor legal and government reporting requirements, and is responsible for the preparation of information requested or required for compliance with laws. Approves all information submitted.

Employee Relations

- Oversees the implementation of Human Resources programs through Human Resources staff. Monitors administration to established standards and procedures. Identifies opportunities for improvement, and resolves any discrepancies.

- Creates, monitors, and advises managers in the progressive discipline system. In partnership with department heads, monitors the implementation of performance improvement process with nonperforming employees.

- Reviews and guides department heads about recommendations for employment terminations. Participates in partnership with Administrator, CFO, CNE, and/or department heads in investigations. Abides by zero tolerance for abuse and state and federal mandated laws.

■ Conducts investigations when employee complaints or concerns are brought forth. Reviews employee appeals through the complaint procedure. Participates with Administrator and CNE in union-related grievances.

Recruitment and Staffing

■ Establishes and leads the standard recruiting and hiring practices and procedures necessary to recruit and hire a superior workforce.

■ Oversees pre-employment screening, pre-employment physical, TB testing requirements, and mandated background checks.

Compensation/Benefits Administration

■ Establishes wage and salary structure, leads competitive market research to pay practices and pay bands that help recruit and retain superior staff.

■ Comonitors with Controller all pay practices and systems for effectiveness and cost containment.

■ Works with CFO, obtains cost-effective employee benefits; monitors national benefits environment for options and cost savings.

There are different theories on the amount of detail to include in a job posting. Some theories say that less is more when writing a job posting or ad.

On the other hand there is the argument that job seekers should know exactly what the job entails so that they can judge whether it is a good fit for them and whether it is what they are looking for. You can determine which method is better for your particular situation, position being posted, and your company's policies or practices.

Required Skills for the HR Manager

Example

- **Education:** Most, but not all, of these occupations require a four-year bachelor's degree.
- **Overall Experience:** A minimum of two to four years of work-related skill, knowledge, or experience is needed for these occupations.
- **Relevant Job Experience:** Usually need several years of work-related experience, on-the-job training, and/or vocational training.

The requirements of the job will dictate the level of experience needed to perform the position you are posting. If there is a company policy regarding certain levels of employment requiring a particular education level, than you will have to comply with the policy. If you have a Human Resources department, check out the company's policies, procedures, and practices.

How to Apply

One advantage of posting on the Internet is that there are several options available to use in your application process and how you would prefer the applicant contact you. If you do not want phone calls you can either state "no calls please" or leave off the phone number.

Guidelines for contact information to be given to the applicant:

- **The type of résumé format required** – Specify MS Word or ASCII.

- **E-mail contact** – Use one or more e-mail addresses for tracking purposes.

- **Phone number** – You may or may not want to include a phone number.

- **Fax number** – Include one, if that is acceptable.

- **Web site** – Having an application process on the company Web site is very convenient for you and the applicant. It is also more reassuring to the applicant that you have a legitimate business and opening.

Posting a Job Online

The World Wide Web is the most comprehensive outreach to candidates that is currently available. You can post jobs online and receive résumés from thousands of potential employees who are searching for jobs online. That then becomes your best tool for recruiting. That's the good news.

How to Write a Successful Job Posting or Ad

The bad news is that you may be overwhelmed with electronic résumés from all over the world. How you handle these résumés is a topic for another book. But be aware that most companies, at least the larger ones, use electronic screening systems to weed out those résumés that are sent to all job postings, whether the senders are qualified or interested or not.

There are many ways of using online Web sites and job boards; here are some suggestions:

- Start with your own company or organization's Web site. Place a link to a specific place on your Web site that shows career opportunities. Persons searching for businesses with your type of product or services will search through companies and will be interested in what potential opportunities your company has to offer. There is no additional cost associated with this posting.

- Classified ads should not be dismissed. There are still those who prefer to search the want ads for openings. The cost is a very reasonable investment.

- Internet resources are available at little or no cost in some cases. An example of such a service is America's Job Bank, which is the busiest job market on the Web. Postings on the site include federal, state, and local jobs in all 50 states. Thousands of employers use this service for their online postings. The cost to do so is low or free.

- Online postings at colleges and universities are available to students and to alumni. Whether you are seeking new grads or seasoned professionals, postings on these sites may be of interest to you. Use is usually free, or there may be a small membership fee.

■ Contact professionals through their association Web sites. Candidates are strongly encouraged to use these sites for their search so they are assured use. The cost of use is either free or very low.

■ Discussion forums for specific industries are sites where there is a great deal of interaction by the users. To post on these sites may involve a cost.

The big job boards such as Monster.com are the most expensive way to post on the Web, but they may be worth the investment, as the outreach and reputation of such boards are extensive. These Web sites usually have an advanced résumé search that will allow you to fine-tune your search.

If you do decide to use the Internet to post your job, your posting *must* be focused so that you attract the right candidates. Once again, the time you take to write your posting will be a worthwhile investment, which should reap big benefits.

Miscellaneous Information

You can add several types of information to your posting regarding benefits, salary, and other types of special opportunities that your position has.

Your company may also wish to post specific qualifiers such a "U.S. Citizenship required, or information about equal opportunity." How you approach this matter will be a choice of style and company practice and policy.

Further discussion about miscellaneous information is given in Chapter 11.

Ten Reasons Why Job Postings Are a Great Recruiting Tool

1. Job postings are quick and easy for both you and the applicant to use.

2. You can manage the postings by trying various versions to see which one works best.

3. There is usually no limit to the words you can use in your posting. Even when there are restrictions, they tend to be generous.

4. You can be specific about exactly what format you want the applicants to use for résumés: MS Word or ASCII.

5. You can use creative thinking to put some drama in your posting to attract the right candidates.

6. You can provide a Web address for your company's Web site, and the prospective applicants can connect directly to the site.

7. You can write any disclaimers regarding the job qualifications, to filter out those candidates who are not serious or not qualified.

8. You can be as descriptive as you want about your company, the culture, and the job duties.

9. You can add a quiz or an assignment to be filled out and submitted along with the application.

10. Job postings are inexpensive—most of the time.

Part Five

The Job Description: Performance Management

A good performance management process begins with a planning session and then continues as an ongoing discussion throughout the year.

If your company does not have a formal performance appraisal or goals measurement system, the job description can be used as a vehicle for you to set expectations. You will find the job description a very efficient method of setting realistic goals with employees. You can then use these goals as a benchmark for tracking performance to determine if those workers are performing up to the standards set.

Chapter 9

Setting Goals

A s discussed in Chapter 1, the job description is the foundation of the job. The foundation is the base, and it should be built upon to complete the structure. How does that work?

The Perfect Scenario

Jack is attracted to a job posting he sees online. The job looks very interesting, and the posting is very clear in defining the job and information about the company and the culture.

He applies per the instructions on the posting and receives a call the very next day. After an initial screening he is asked to come in for an interview.

He interviews successfully a few times, and then he is asked to meet with the hiring manager to discuss the position and, he hopes, an offer.

The discussion focuses around the job description and the responsibilities outlined in the description. There are many questions from both the hiring manager and Jack to clarify the meaning of some of the duties and responsibilities.

The process has begun. There is agreement regarding the duties and responsibilities of the job. Jack has a sense of what will be expected of him, and the hiring manager knows that he has been forthright in laying out expectations.

Jack receives an offer and feels good about the process so far, particularly the communication and expectations laid out. He accepts the offer, and will begin the job in two weeks.

When Jack arrives at the new job he is greeted warmly and is made to feel welcome from his first encounter with the receptionist to the introduction of the new staff with whom he will be working.

The hiring manager makes it a point to visit Jack's cubicle and ask Jack if he can schedule a meeting for the two of them to meet after lunch. Jack agrees.

In the meeting that afternoon Jack is supplied with a copy of the job description used during his interview. This version has notes jotted in the margin by the hiring manager.

The discussion starts where it left off during the interview. The responsibilities and duties of the position now are accompanied by percentages and more detail. Jack is asked for his opinion and is also asked for buy-in to the goals.

Jack leaves the meeting feeling like he has his work cut out for him. He also leaves with a sense that his boss has taken over two hours to set up goals with him and set out expectations of completion.

He also feels that the support of his hiring manager is with him. They have just made a verbal contract of commitment to accomplish a set of goals that Jack has agreed to.

Jack is eager and ready to take on his new challenges.

In this ideal scenario the hiring manager has used the job description to set out the goals and lay the foundation of the work expectations for Jack's next few weeks. There will be follow-up meetings to make sure Jack is on track and not floundering, but there will be no need to micromanage, as Jack has the "map" of where is he going and how he is expected to get there.

The first thing articles about how to write an employee performance review usually begin with is advice to have meetings with your employee at least once a month. That's a good idea. But what the articles don't tell you about is that that first meeting should take place during the first week the new employee begins.

That initial meeting is when the expectations are laid out that can be discussed in your monthly meetings. Setting the goals is very important to the success of any employee. What is expected? How can anyone do a great job if it's not known what is expected of him or her?

Writing an effective job description takes some work. But by investing that time up front, you can reap the benefits by using your work to define what you need and want from your new employee.

Goals are not written in stone; they may have to be adjusted to fit the situation or circumstances. But, without a goal, employees do not know what is expected of them and when they are expected to deliver. Goals should be flexible and be changed if something is not working as planned.

Meeting on a regular basis and documenting what has been said is a great way to guarantee a solid performance review from you at the end of the cycle. One of the pitfalls of almost everyone is that we remember only recent events. So if an employee starts off with a strong performance and then cools off a bit, by the time the performance review comes around the manager can only remember the last few months or even weeks and forget about what a great start the employee had.

The job description will become a great communication tool between you and your employees to assure that you are both "singing from the same hymn book."

Perfect Plan for the Perfect First Performance Review Meeting

The first performance management meeting should take place as soon as possible after a new employee begins work. Preparation should be done to ensure that the meeting is focused and that you are prepared to lead the dialogue. What's needed?

The Materials

- New employee's résumé and application
- Job description used to hire the employee
- Department goals (if available)
- Company mission statement (if available), company goals, or any other information about the culture or the purpose of the business of the company
- Company organizational chart (if available)
- Expectations that you have for this position
- Benchmarking (the results desired for this position as compared to average or above-average performance)

The Meeting

Be sure to give the new employee adequate notice before the meeting. Ask the employee to prepare any thoughts on the position and how that worker sees himself or herself fitting in and accomplishing the goals of the position.

Set aside an allotted time of one to two hours in a secluded meeting place where you will not be interrupted. If your office is the only place available, make sure all phones are turned off or forwarded to voice mail.

It is important that you give your full attention to this meeting. It will set the tone for the future of this employee and his or her time in this position.

When you sit down with the new employee, attempt to make him or her feel as comfortable as possible. Start with some small talk about the new job and how it is going so far.

Ask about the commute or the adjustments being made by the employee. Talk for a few minutes about the company and your experience or your beginning days at the company.

Begin the formal part of the meeting by stating the purpose of laying out the expectations of the position and setting benchmarks of success along the way. Be sure to emphasize that this is a two-way conversation and that you expect the employee to contribute or ask any questions that he or she may have.

Next discuss the job description and levels of importance of the various duties and responsibilities. This would be a good point to add percentages for the importance of each duty.

Example

- Coordinates between departments and customers to organize projects and complete writing assignments. (15%)

- Creates and revises processes and documentation, including systems and associated databases. (30%)

- Creates, writes, and revises technical system training materials. (25%)

- Reviews and revises existing documentation for consistency and accuracy based on current best practices. (20%)

- Confers with customers, vendors, and executives to ensure that specifications are correct and agreed upon. (10%)

It is extremely important that there be a clear understanding between you and the employee as to where the proportions of time should be spent. If the employee thinks that conferring with customers and vendors is the most important part of the position, and he or she focuses attention there, that person will be very surprised at your dissatisfaction with the job performance, because he or she has had success with the coordinating and conferring goal. That employee differs with you about what is important in this role; in this case, writing and revising are deemed more important.

The communication at the initial meeting is rather commonsense and basic, but if the meeting does not take place, there can be a great deal of misunderstanding about the expectations of the employee. Small things have a way of turning into big things if they are not dealt with from the very start of the job.

Throughout the course of the meeting, continue to discuss the various duties and the measures of excellence for performance or benchmarking. If possible, set dates or quantities for the goals. The more specific you can get, the better.

Benchmarking and setting specific goals are easier to do for jobs that have concrete results, such as sales positions. It is more difficult to benchmark and gauge success for someone in areas with less concrete results—in the Human Resources (HR) department, for example. The HR person is dealing with people and problems, and it is more of a challenge in that situation to quantify success. The measures of success are less concrete, but they may show up in better employee morale or less turnover of employees.

Standards set at the initial meeting should be discussed on a regular basis and adjusted accordingly. If possible, set up a regular meeting time on a weekly, monthly, or quarterly basis.

During each meeting you should require input from the employee about the assessment of his or her performance and the satisfaction level that person is experiencing. These meetings should stay very focused and not become a dumping or complaining session. Topics should focus on results and problems or obstacles and how to work on improving conditions and performance.

To be worthwhile, any performance management system needs to be ongoing. If you plan to meet with employees only once a year for the annual performance appraisal, you will miss out on the rewards of communication, and your employees may become disgruntled at the surprises they hear at a once-a-year meeting.

There should be no surprises about performance. The communication must be ongoing and clear. If there are problems, this is a method to stop negative behaviors before they become too set to change.

There seems to be more of a tendency to pass up these communication opportunities if the performance is good or above average. "They already perform well, why would we need to discuss their performance?" a boss said. This is the wrong approach if the goal is to retain this employee. A bit of encouragement and positive feedback is always appreciated, even from the star performers.

Companies that have performance plans connected to career development plans are far more successful in retaining good employees. If there are plans and goals to work toward, employees are more likely to stay.

The Job Description: Performance Management

One of the main reasons most people seek employment in new companies is that they are looking for a "challenge." Having a performance plan geared toward growth, development, and eventually a guided career path keeps the employee more focused and satisfied.

Chapter 10

Measuring Performance: Benchmarks of Performance

Benchmarking began in the manufacturing field, where companies could define what was the "best" by comparing one thing against another. The process was primarily used for re-engineering or quality improvement.

The computer industry has used benchmarking to assess the relative performance of an object and running a number of standard tests and trials against it.

Here's a concise definition of *benchmarking*:

The process of evaluating and comparing organizational processes and systems against those that are rated best in the industry.

This process usually involves collecting, analyzing, and reporting critical operational data. Benchmarking helps to identify the operational areas in need of improvement. It also compares the effectiveness of a process or method with that of the competitors.

If we take this idea of collecting, analyzing, and reporting critical operational data, and then comparing it, not to the competition but against goals set, what we have is a new way to use benchmarking in performance management.

Let's return to Jack's ideal scenario, which was discussed in Chapter 9:

Jack has worked for the company for four weeks now, and he and the hiring manager have met at least once a week. During those meetings, they have tracked the beginning of Jack's efforts to work against his list of tasks defined in the job description from the first meeting that took place.

His hiring manager and he have the one-month meeting scheduled for this week. Jack has taken the job description and listed the responsibilities and the duties of the job and the goals that were set in the first week on the job. He has been tracking his progress against those goals. He is very satisfied with the progress he has been able to measure.

His hiring manager begins the first-month meeting by asking Jack how he is liking the job so far. He also asks Jack how he feels he is doing. Jack answers that his expectations have been surpassed by the job so far; he feels that he is making great progress based on the goals set from the very beginning. The hiring manager then gives Jack excellent feedback, and the two spend the rest of the time reviewing Jack's progress.

During that time, some adjustments are made to the goals, and there is some discussion about the benchmarks that have been set as a standard for Jack's performance. He is doing well, but there are areas he will want to focus on to improve.

By the end of the first year of employment, Jack has had 12 such meetings with his hiring manager. When the time comes for the performance appraisal, that meeting is quite easy for both of them.

During the past 11 months, Jack and his manager have been collecting, analyzing, and reporting critical operational data, and they have a real sense of what Jack can and cannot do. They have benchmarked Jack's progress.

They will set new goals and perhaps add to the duties and responsibilities, depending on Jack's progress.

With the job description used as a tool for performance management, you can benchmark progress of your employee while improving communications. There will be a stronger sense of accomplishment than there would have been if you had just checked off boxes for "satisfactory" or "above expectations." There will be real data to compare performance.

Benchmarking

Wikipedia defines benchmarking as...

The process of comparing the cost, cycle time, productivity, or quality of a specific process or method to another that is widely considered to be an industry standard or best practice. Essentially, benchmarking provides a snapshot of the performance of your business and helps you understand where you are in relation to a particular standard.

The result is often a business case for making changes in order to make improvements.

Benchmarking is most [often] used to measure performance using a specific indicator (e.g., cost per unit of measure, productivity per unit of measure, cycle time of x per unit of measure, or defects per unit of measure) resulting in a metric of performance that is then compared to others.

Part Six

If you look at various job descriptions and the formats used, you will see some terms that turn up frequently but not necessarily consistently.

When you write your job description you may want to read through the various terms to see if any of them apply to your situation in your company.

Chapter 11

Special Phrases

Open-Ended Responsibilities

You sometimes may want to leave the job responsibilities open until you have hired the new employee. You can then add tasks and responsibilities when you meet with the employee to discuss expectations. Flexibility is especially important, as you may find that the new employee has special skills that may be used in addition to the normal responsibilities of the job. For instance, he or she may speak a foreign language.

Here are some examples of phrases that leave the job responsibilities open:

NOTE: This job description is not intended to be all-inclusive. Employee may perform other related duties as negotiated to meet the ongoing needs of the organization.

The essentials of the position include, but are not limited to, the following duties ...

Equal Opportunity: Government Compliance

Not every job description includes terms relating to "equal opportunity," but it is a requirement of federal law that every employer abide by the rules of the Fair Labor Standards Act (FLSA). The Act encompasses the following regulations and organizations:

Equal Employment Opportunity (EEO)

Americans with Disabilities Act (ADA)

Family and Medical Leave Act (FMLA)

Employee Retirement Income Security Act (ERISA)

Department of Labor (DOL)

Worker's Compensation

Occupational Safety and Health Administration (OSHA)

Health Insurance Portability and Accountability Act (HIPPA) laws

"Equal opportunity" is a very important phrase to include in your job description if your organization is a government contractor or receives any funding from the government; for example:

We Are an Equal Opportunity Employer
Equal Opportunity Employer M/F/D/V
(male, female, disabled, veteran)
Working Safely is a Condition of Employment at CFT— An Affirmative Action Employer M/F/D/V

Special Condition of Employment

While it is unlawful to discriminate based on the country of origin, certain jobs require U.S. citizenship due to the nature of the work performed. Government contractors, or those who work in highly sensitive or classified areas of government jobs, would be affected by this phrase:

> U.S. CITIZENSHIP REQUIRED. Applicants selected for some positions will be subjected to a government security investigation and will need to meet eligibility requirements for access to classified information.

Requirement of Employment

Some positions have special requirements that would best be described before any interviewing takes place. Doing so will ensure that there are no misunderstandings once the person is hired. The condition should be spelled out clearly, as it is in these examples:

Successful candidates must be available to travel and work in excess of standard hours when necessary.

Valid New Mexico's driver's license required with acceptable driving record for past three years.

Ability to lift up to 50 lbs.

Must possess, or be able to attain before actual Hire Date, a Loan Originator's license issued by the State Department of Financial Institutions.

Benefits and Other Attractions

By including in the job description the benefits your company offers, you entice the job seeker to look further. Not all companies choose to include benefits; it is a matter of style and choice. Here are some examples of benefits mentioned in a job description:

Excellent salary for the right candidate $55–$75K. Full health insurance after 90 days.

We offer an excellent starting salary, great benefits, and room for advancement.

At Happy Company we offer an outstanding array of benefits and a competitive salary that upholds our commitment to excellent employee care. EOE

Competitive base and incentive plan as well as a comprehensive benefits package, including medical, dental, vision, life and disability, 401(k) Savings Plan, and paid time off.

What we Offer:

- *Competitive salaries*
- *Medical, dental, vision, 401(k), and other benefits*
- *Energetic, focused, and collaborative work environment*

Offers excellent benefits including health, dental, vision, company paid life insurance, 401(k) with company contributions, tuition reimbursement, flexible spending accounts, paid vacation, and the opportunity for personal and professional growth.

Salary Information

The matter of providing salary information in your posting is somewhat controversial.

On one hand, you entice those who are qualified and don't want to waste time if the salary isn't up to their expectations. On the other hand, you may turn people off who think the salary is too low or too high for their particular skills and qualifications.

You will have to determine the pluses for the position you are posting in accordance with your company's policy on compensation.

Here are terms relating to salary information that are included in some job postings:

Compensation Package:

Salary Range: $70,000– $75,000 with the best benefits.

Annual salary range is currently $100,000–$130,000, with excellent benefits package, including 4/10 work schedule and company car.

Instructions on How to Apply

Many online posting sites include a link that will allow the applicant to go directly to a company's Web site to apply. Some employers choose to give out a particular person's e-mail address where résumés can be sent, and others prefer to use regular mail.

How you want to receive applications should be spelled out so that the job seeker will know exactly how to proceed to contact you.

These are some typical phrases used in job postings to direct the job applicant to respond:

If you are interested in this opportunity, please take a moment to review the position on our Web site: www.companyname.com.

If you are interested in this job opportunity, please e-mail a current résumé in WORD doc format to: name@emailaddress.com.

Please submit your résumé, along with salary requirements, to: name@gmail.com.

If you require further details, feel free to call me at 677–555–4555.

For additional questions, please contact Jane Doe, Human Resources Manager, at jdoe@humanresources.com.

For a detailed recruitment brochure, containing additional compensation information and application instructions, please visit our Web site at www.brochure.com.

Special Mission Statements

Some companies have special statements that indicate the culture at the company and the philosophy toward employee service. This is an option that is open to you if you have a special mission or statement that you would want to include.

Here are some examples of such statements:

We believe in serving employees first. If we take care of our employees, then those employees will take care of our customers.

We strongly believe in recognizing those who exemplify excellence, and reward them for contributing to our collective success. From individual to department to spontaneous recognition—we find unique ways to thank our employees for the outstanding efforts they make every day.

Top Ten Mistakes When Writing Job Descriptions

1. Adding fluff and padding to the job description. No fluff allowed! Keep it simple and straightforward.

2. Writing uninspiring job descriptions—boring! No one will read beyond the first sentence.

3. Not being specific with details—this is no place for vague or misleading language.

4. Being overzealous in what the position can accomplish—this is "wishful thinking" but not realistic.

5. Not reviewing what has been done in the past—interviewing someone who is leaving the position.

6. Not thinking about what you want in the new candidate—before the search process begins.

7. Not targeting the job to the right job seeker; failure to entice or excite the right candidate.

8. Writing "tasks-only" job descriptions. Devoting more than 75 percent of the job description to this one area is too much.

9. Losing sight of the fact that this is a "recruiting tool"—make it look like an interesting opportunity.

10. Using a cut and paste job description from another company as your job description for your company culture.

About the Author

Carole Martin is a coach with over 18 years' experience in Human Resources Management in various industries: Biotechnology, Aerospace, Software Engineering, Sales, Publishing, and Consulting. She is an acknowledged expert in the use of behavioral interviewing techniques and has made interviewing her specialty.

Carole has been recognized as an interview expert on sev eral TV shows and has been a guest on numerous radio shows including international shows in Canada and the UK. She is quoted frequently in newspapers and magazines including *New York Times, LA Times; Men's Health, Women's Health, HR Magazine, Smart Money, Parents magazine, Employment Management Today, Details, Wall Street Journal.com, Employment Review, Self Magazine, Marie Claire magazine,* and *RT Image.*

Carole holds a master's degree in Career Development from John F. Kennedy University in Pleasant Hill, CA, where she is an adjunct faculty member, teaching interviewing skills to counselors. She has been an adjunct coach at Haas Business School in Berkeley for the past eight years, has worked with the MBA students at Washington University in St. Louis, and also works for UCLA.

Carole has been certified by The Human Resources Certification Institute as a Senior Professional in Human Resources (SPHR). Additionally, she has authored five books on job search and interviewing: *Interview Fitness Training, Boost Your Interview IQ, Perfect Phrases for the Perfect Interview, Boost Your Hiring IQ,* and *The Complete Book of Perfect Phrases for Successful Job Seekers.*

Her Web site is www.interviewcoach.com.

The Right Phrase for Every Situation...Every Time.